The Last Days at High School:

Forcados High School

O.B Adewale

ISBN: 9798848784688

DEDICATION

To God Almighty

CONTENTS

CHAPTER 1

It was early in the morning and still dark when Jimi Solade woke up to someone shaking him roughly. He groaned and mumbled to himself, half asleep. Jimi!' He jerked fully awake at the sound of that familiar voice. It was his brother. 'Wole!' Jimi said in surprise. ‘Yes, it's me,' and his brother smiled in a way that showed only his upper teeth. ‘Man! What...?' Jimi began. They looked at each other, delighted. ‘No greeting, little bro?' Wole smiled again. 'Sorry, does anyone know you're here? Does Daddy...?' Jimi did not complete the sentence; instead, he embraced his brother tightly. I've missed you!' Wole was thinner. Jimi could feel it. 'Mum knows I'm here,' Wole said. He too did not mention their father. Just then, the alarm clock sounded. It was time for Jimi to get up and he released his brother. 'Go on, get ready for school,'

Wole said, stretching on the bed. At least you seem happy to see me.' He looked round the room at the carelessly flung shirts, jeans and boxer shorts over the chair, to the poster of the Manchester United football team on the wall above Jimi's bed. A typical boy's room. Another worn-out poster of Tupac Shakur was pasted on the opposite wall. 'I didn't remove it even though it's an eyesore,' Jimi said, grinning. 'Everything's just as you left it.' Wole squeezed Jimi's arm lightly. He picked up something from the bedside table beside Jimi's music CDs, chemistry and mathematics textbooks. 'Man, this is some watch. Must have cost a mountain. You always get all the nicest things, why...?' 'Wole, don't touch my watch. 'What's your problem? Can't I look at a watch?' I'm sorry bro,' Jimi muttered. ‘I'm glad to see you back- really- but, you know...'My cute, spoilt little brother... You grow taller every time I see you.' Wole got up walked towards the door. 'Don't worry about the old bear. Better get ready for school. Er-I took some cash from your drawer, hope you don't mind? Sighing, Jimi plodded to the bathroom. Trust his brother to always collect things, but he was happy he was back. It was a new day and the beginning of his final year at school. Like his brother, he was as tall and long-limbed as an athlete, though, unlike his brother, he had dimples when he smiled. He was sixteen years old and he was already sprouting a beard. He flexed his right arm noting that he had developed muscles. Good. He whistled as he took his shower, refusing to think about the morning's surprise. The reason why was a long story; too long to think about on a brand-new day.

***

As Jimi ate his breakfast of moin-moin and brown pap, Wole sat on the sofa watching early morning cartoons on television. Their mother was in the kitchen with Risikat, their househelp. It was like any other morning - peaceful, almost as if Wole had never left. Then Mr. Solade came out of his bedroom, yawning. He was a tall and well-built man with a head shaved bald. He wore a loose caftan over his bulging tummy. 'Kemi...' he began and then stopped short and rubbed his eyes, and rubbed them again just to make sure. 'Good morning, Papa,' Wole said and, as an afterthought, prostrated himself. He sounded as if he was enjoying himself. What are you doing here?' his father said in a strangled voice. Mrs. Solade came running out of the kitchen. 'Good morning, dear. Just relax and let me explain...' Jimi knew his father wouldn't listen. ‘What is this good-for-nothing doing in my house?' his father roared. 'Didn't I tell you never to set foot in here again? Get out before I call the police!' 'Kola!' Mrs. Solade shouted-if her high, thin voice could be called a shout. 'It's too early in the morning for this. And he is your son! You cannot treat him like this! You must not go on like this! She knelt down. It's you!' Mr. Solade turned on her. 'You spoiled the boy! He has brought shame and disgrace on this family and you still beg for him. All your children are bad!' Jimi jumped down from the dining table and knelt down too, beside his mother and brother. 'Papa, forgive him.' Mr. Solade stood still, his chest heaving, and said very quietly, 'You are not welcome here,' and turned back to his room. Mrs. Solade collapsed onto a chair, but when Wole stood up, he was grinning widely. 'You can laugh,' his mother said. 'It's not funny. You saw how he reacted. We shall have to see Uncle Kazeem and maybe Uncle Shola. They will talk to him.' 'He's not a serious man,' Wole said, grinning. 'Ah, Wole!' his mother protested. 'He's your father!' Jimi picked up his schoolbag and slung it over his shoulder. 'You've not finished eating,' his mother said anxiously. ‘I'm not hungry. Bro, stay cool.' He was annoyed as he turned for the door, but he didn't know exactly why. Papa and his temper, Jimi thought. Outside the gate, he stood for a moment and listened to the distant sounds of the buses and shouts of the bus conductors on the main road. A cock crowed in the distance. Someone called his name. It was his next-door neighbour and schoolmate, Ansa Izaegbegbe, running towards him. A short, thin boy who hardly reached Jimi's shoulders. 'Heard you arrived back from your trip yesterday, Ansa said, slightly out of breath. ‘Was waiting for you.' 'Hey Ansaboy! Sorry. My mind was somewhere else.' Jimi smiled delightedly and threw Ansa a friendly punch. Ansa snorted noisily. "Well, it's nice to have you back."

CHAPTER 2

Jimi and Ansa got to school just before assembly was due to start. Jimi left to join the other prefects. Morning assembly took place in the large hall that stood in the centre of the school and students lined up according to their classes. The school band, looking smart as always, had positioned itself in one corner and was already beating drums softly in practice. A few teachers were waiting outside the hall, ready to punish latecomers by asking them to kneel down. At eight o'clock, Seyi Lawal, the head boy, stood up on the stage. He was fat and smooth-cheeked from the holidays and, with his hand on his chest, he smiled with faint smugness. He loved his job. Attention everybody!' hc called out. "The National Anthem.' The school band struck up the tune, drums beating, and the students raggedly joined in. The juniors were eager and enthusiastic, the seniors uninterested. All the students of

Forcados High School were excited to be back after the long, long summer break. The school held an unofficial pride of place among all the other schools in the area: it had the largest football field and the best layout. Bright purple and orange bougainvillea had been carefully planted along the fences. The school buildings were arranged in small one- and two-storey blocks, with rows of hibiscus plants forming small hedges between each class. Others often said that Forcados students were 'artificial,' but the school took pride in the fact that it always defeated other schools in regional quizzes and sports. After the national anthem and assembly prayers Mallam, the principal, gave a brief talk welcoming eve He was a small, wiry man with an odd accent, as if he spoke through his nose. The students loved imitating him. as a pleasure to have all of you back. It is very import however that we face up to the responsibilities of this term particularly our final year students who have the West Africa Examination Council (WAEC) examinations. This is an important watershed... When assembly was over, the students boys in white shirts, black ties and black trousers, and girls in black pinafores over white shirts- crowded into the hallways and corridors of the school, chatting Some people greeted Ansa, but many more crowded around Jimi. 'Jimi, where have you been?' 'Missed you! 'Conchie's annoyed! 'Party tonight... Jimi was soon lost in laughter and chatter. Forgotten, Ansa looked around glumly. The first days of term were always the worst, Back to further math's and physics, and everyone talking in the latest slang about what they'd been up to and what new music was out, while he had nothing to say, He saw that some students wore their ties in odd knots and had chains on their trousers, showing off watches and shoes, American bling-bling. Some also carried the latest Nokia or Samsung cell phones even though students weren't allowed to use phones There were the same old people: the gorilla like Okoro, a miserable bully, Teacher Bade, whom students called cane, was always waiting for the next hapless kid who would fall into his trap, the Rhymers a group of five boys who composed hip-hop lyrics after school, hoping to become the next Nigerian sensation; Eze the bright spark who was in an unspoken contest with Jimi over their chemistry results, and finally, gum chewing Caro (Jimi's Caro, or the other way round), the Queen Bee with her perpetually disdainful expression. Ansa could never understand what his friend saw in her Jimi was the best student in chemistry and a whiz kid in other subjects. He had won prizes and laurels for the school in science and debate competitions. He was also the health prefect, the athletic club captain and the best footballer. What's more, all the girls thought he was good-looking. If there was anyone who could be described as an all-rounder, it was Jimi Solade. Some people have all the luck, thought Ansa. but Jimi was such a friendly, likeable person that people were hardly envious of him. It had always been like that. For instance, Mama Silifat, who sold puff-puff and akara outside the school premises, would always give Jimi the largest pieces, smiling and calling him by his full name, Akinjimi, or omo mi (my child). Jimi had been Ansa's hero since primary school because he was good at so many things, while the only thing Ansa knew how to do was paint. There had never been two friends who were more different. A plump girl with short plaits framing her round, gentle face came over. It was Nene Ekpo. She lived on the same street as Jimi and Ansa and she was one of their oldest friends. Ansa was genuinely glad to see her. She had the sweetest smile. ‘Hi Ansa!" she said in her light, pretty voice. 'Glad to see you. Look at Jims, when did he get back?' ‘He came back yesterday.' ‘I could hear his voice from a distance, rowdy and full of fun as usual,' said Nene, laughing. 'By the way, do you remember anyone called Efua? She's a relative of Mrs. Alli who lives on Balogun Street, not too far from us. Ansa wrinkled his forehead. 'No, I don't.' Neither do 1-not very well. She was at our primary school for a while and she's coming here to join us. In SS3?' ‘I think she had to leave her former school-at least that's what her aunt told my mother. Her aunt asked me-us rather -to help her settle down and get used to things. How were your holidays?' ‘Oh, boring. But I did get the opportunity to go to an art workshop for one week.' 'Sounds like fun.' She turned toward Jimi. ‘Jimi’s! Hello!'

***

After school, Jimi walked behind a block of classrooms. It was empty there and closest to the back wall of the school. Several huge Casuarina trees loomed there and, except for the occasional rustling of a lizard against leaves or the soft cooing of a laughing dove, all was quiet. Jimi put on his earphones and turned on his iPod until loud hip-hop music filled his ears. They hadn't done much schoolwork today: he and the other prefects had to mobilise the students, mostly juniors, to pick leaves and do other chores, and he now wanted to be alone. It was rare for Jimi to be or want to be alone, but he had a lot of things on his mind. Wole had returned. There was a time when he and his brother had been very close, standing together against the savage bullying of their oldest brother, Femi, but Wole had changed. He had been expelled from two different schools and kicked out of university for reasons Jimi didn't fully understand. The last time Wole had been home he had falsified his father's signature and made away with a lot of money. That was something Papa Solade could never forgive-never. He had been so furious when he discovered Jimi and Wole still saw each other secretly that he had even sent Jimi away to Ibadan for the holidays. He said he didn't want Jimi under Wole's bad influence. Now, his father was increasingly in a bad mood, growling at everyone and blaming Mrs. Solade for spoiling them-as if Jimi had ever done anything bad; not like Wole anyway. His mother too seemed tired and harassed all the time. ‘I'm just not feeling too good, it's nothing to worry about, really,' she'd say. Jimi had decided nothing was going to bother him again. It was time for school and he was going to keep on being the brightest student, getting the best results in WAEC, while still partying, playing football and enjoying the admiration of lots of girls. A sudden movement startled him. It was the head boy, Seyi. ‘Jims, we have a prefect meeting with Mr. Mallum now. As they got to the office, two people came out. One of them was a middle-aged woman dressed in an expensive iro and buba. Her gele was huge! The two boys had to bend their heads slightly to avoid bumping it. She wore dark sunglasses and her mouth was tightly pursed in a grim, forbidding manner. The other was a girl who was not wearing a school uniform. It was a bit difficult to tell what she looked like because she had an odd expression on her face, as if she was going to be sick. 'Who are they?' Seyi asked Jimi. Jimi shrugged, 'Don't know.'

CHAPTER 3

The girl sat quietly in the rickety, jerky taxi, 'Ugh!' her mother said irritably to the driver. This car is so slow--and dirty as well! She turned to her daughter. "Efus, sit straight, you're looking dead. Efus ignored her mother, knowing it would irritate her further. 'Well, I trust we've found a place where even you will find it difficult to get into trouble, her mother said, eyes glittering. The car stopped in front of a grey building. A small, round woman wearing a gold wig and bright red lipstick was standing by the gate. 'Funmil Efual' the woman shrieked. Her mother smiled. 'Moni, this is Efua. Efua's aunt embraced her. Efua stood a little stiffly, somewhat embarrassed at her aunt's warmth. She smelt of a queer but not unpleasant mixture of strong perfume and oranges. 'Such a long time. You remember me? You-' 'All right,' her mother interrupted. 'I'll be off.' 'So soon? You're not getting down? My girl prepared egusi soup and-' 'I have a plane to catch. I'll write you a cheque. Efua, bye-bye and be a good girl. Don't give Aunty Moni any trouble. The taxi sped off and Efua helped her aunt to carry her bags inside. Her aunt kept chatting in a high-pitched voice. 'Forcados is a nice school. They always have excellent results every year. Such a pity you were exp-er, had to leave your former school. I told a few people you were coming.' 'Remember Nene Ekpo? Her father is Pastor Ekpo and she's such a sweet girl...' Later that day, as Efua was in her room unpacking, she heard her aunt calling shrilly, 'Efua, come out and meet someone!' Oh dear, Efua thought. She took a deep breath and went out. Nene and her mother had dropped by. 'Nene, this is my niece Efua Coker, Aunt Moni said. 'Efua, this is Mrs. Ekpo and her daughter, Nene." Nene stared at Efua. She'd had a hazy memory of her and she had been expecting-well, she wasn't sure what she had been expecting- but certainly not the girl standing in front of her. Efua was tall and slender, with large eyes and long eyelashes. Her hair fell in tangled plaits across her shoulders. She had a delicate, mysterious beauty that made Nene think of a freshly blossoming flower. She certainly didn't look like someone capable of being expelled. ‘Good afternoon,' Efua greeted her visitors, curtseying a little. She had a surprisingly deep, almost masculine voice. ‘Come here, you pretty child,' Mrs. Ekpo sang out. I hear you will be going to the same school as my daughter. Hello,' Nene said, feeling a little awkward. 'I don't think you'll remember me; I'm afraid I don't much remember you. Why don't you both step outside and talk?' Aunt Moni suggested. The girls stepped out to the balcony. I'm a commercial student,' Nene began. 'What class do you attend?' 'Science." ‘Oh, you're a brainy one.

Well, I suppose it doesn't matter whether we're in different classes. Let me tell you a little about our school. Morning assembly starts by eight, so I'll come over at seven-thirty, if you like. You must plait your hair in the week's style. I'll show you where I do mine.' ‘I'd like that very much, thank you. ‘So tell me about your former school. Girls only, wasn't it? Forcados is mixed - it may come as a shock. 'I hope not,' said Efun. They both laughed, suddcnly discovering they liked each other. Nene continued, 'Do you remember two boys called Ansa and Jimi?' Efua frowned. I think I do. Very troublesome boys, am I right?’ ‘Only one of them was.' They laughed again. ‘I hope you'll like it here', Nene said.

***

The next day, as the students stood in front of the hall laughing and talking just before assembly, Jimi joined the other prefects trying to organise everybody into lines. ‘No more chains on trousers or dangling earrings for the girls. There will be an inspection of fingernails and socks during assembly. Principal's orders, he said. Then he noticed Nene standing with an unfamiliar girl. Efua clung close to Nene. She felt queasy, the object of curious attention. Jimi moved over to Ansa. 'Who's that girl, the one with Nene?' 'Oh, that must be the new girl she was telling me about yesterday, Ansa said.

'A new student is joining us?' 'Strange, isn't it? Nene said she once attended our primary school, so she might recognise us. Ef-something, um- yes, Efua, Efua. Jimi had never heard of her, but she looked rather former school. Well, Jimi Solade to the rescue. nice-not bright, though. She had probably failed at her 'Come on, he said, half dragging Ansa. 'Let Nene introduce us: Ansa sighed; he knew Jimi very well. ‘Hello Nene,' said

Jimi. ‘Efua, these are the boys I was telling you about. Jimi and Ansa,’ Nene said. 'Boys, this is Efua Coker'. Ansa murmured awkwardly; he always felt shy around girls. Jimi just stared, his mouth open a little, until Nene prodded him. ‘Jimi!' ‘Oh, I'm sorry,' he said. He stretched to his full height, flashed his brightest Mr. Cool smile and extended his hand. ‘I'm Jimi Solade. Nice to meet you, although we're supposed to have met before. Efua stared at him, not taking his hand. 'I remember you,' she said frostily. "You once put a dead lizard on my table. “Oh, Jimi was flustered. 'I don't recall... Yes-but you were just kids,' said Efua. She turned to Nene. ‘Can you show me round a bit?' They both walked off, and Ansa decided he didn't like her at all. Snooty! Just who did she think she was? Jimi still had that dazed expression on his face. At that moment, the bell rang. After classes at the end of the day, Efua walked slowly to the principal's office. It had not been a pleasant day. In the first class, the teacher, Mr. Bade, came in and stopped short at the sight of her. ‘Who are you?' he barked. She stood up and said, I'm Efua Coker, sir,' in her best lady-like manner, the way girls at her former school were taught to speak. ‘What are you doing here?' 'What-excuse me sir, I don't understand. Are you supposed to be in this class? A new student in SS3?' ‘Ye-es.' He gave a snort and ignored her for the rest of the lesson. Each teacher kept saying the same thing: ‘What is your name?' and 'You are new in a senior class?" until she thought she would scream. The math’s teacher, a portly middle-aged woman added, 'I suppose you know what being in this class is all about?' They didn't like her because new students didn't normally come into school at the senior class. They thought she might lower their results. They must have thought she was a bird. brain who had managed to buy her way in. What could she answer to that? The students giggled or whispered and nudged each other. Now, she was supposed to meet the principal and she wasn't looking forward to what he had to say. Mr. Mallum was seated behind his table piled with bulky but neat files. He wore small glasses. 'Miss Coker, you know why you are here?' he began abruptly. Yes, because my mother gave this school an endowment, she said to herself. 'It was difficult for us to accept you and register you for this final year, but we took some factors into consideration. You are a straight-A student and your former headmistress gave you a glowing recommendation, even though she had to expel you after you ran away from school.' Efua bowed her head a little. 'I find it difficult to believe an obviously intelligent young girl like you could...' Efua knew where this conversation was going and decided to take drastic action. 'Oh sir,' she said quietly. 'She tried to make her voice as meek as possible. I'm not a bad girl. I'm really not. I was going through a rebellious phase. I promise you I'll never do anything to make you regret taking me here.' She sniffed a little, hoping it sounded real. The principal stared at Efua. There was something that was not quite right about her, but he could not decide what it was. 'You are under probation for this term. We will be watching your marks closely to know if you can cope and you are to meet the guidance counsellor once a week. Good luck in Forcados. 'Thank you,' Efua said and went out. Once outside, she dropped the meek act. She found a shady spot beneath a mango tree and leaned against the rough bark. The school grounds were deserted now and a small flock of grey and black pigeons strutted and fed on the grass not far from where she stood. Mr. Mallum hadn't been too bad, though she would never have thought he would speak to Mrs. Obange, her former principal. She thought of Mrs. Obange, a large woman with a gruff, friendly voice so different from thin, stuffy Mr. Mallum. The principal hadn't wanted to expel her: What is wrong, Efua? Why did you run away?' Mrs. Obange had asked after Efua had been brought back to the school. But Efua hadn't been ready to open up. ‘You can tell me to leave if you want,' she had replied, defiantly. Mrs. Obange had flared up at that. ‘Very well. If you want to leave, then leave you shall.' She had got what she wanted, hadn't she? She had left Abuja; she was away from her mother and stepfather, and all of them. Suddenly, she couldn't help thinking of her former school, St Catherine's, an all-girls boarding school. She thought of all her friends and clubs, and the busy life she used to lead. At this moment, she thought, the girls would be on their way to the dining hall, forming a long row of blue in their school uniforms... I was a fool, she thought. I only hurt myself. A tear trickled down her face and, suddenly overcome by regret, she burst into tears. The pigeons, startled by the noise, took to the air in a flurry of flapping wings.

CHAPTER 4

Jimi arrived home from school to find his father in a foul temper. ‘Good afternoon, Papa,' Jimi said, but he got no answer. Mrs. Solade whispered to him, looking harassed. ’Daddy’s travelling later this afternoon and we're looking for his case. What do you want to cat?' Jimi had felt very hungry but now his appetite was gone. Anything,' he said and walked to his room. He lay on his bed staring at the faded Tupac postcr. Wole wasn't at home, but it seemed his father was always looking for an excuse to fly into one of his ‘My briefcase,' he heard his father snap. 'Where is it? Not too difficult to guess since we have a thief back here. Only two weeks! A little while later when he heard his mother call, 'Here it is This is it, isn't it?' Jimi came out of his room. His father took the casc and pccred at it closely. ‘It would seem so." ‘See,' she smiled. 'All it needed was a little more careful searching.'

‘Please,' he barked, 'it's all the same! That boy would have taken it if he had seen it. Or maybe he did and you're covering up for him.' 'Don't talk to her like that!' Jimi couldn't believe he had just said that. Mr. Solade stared at him. 'What did you say?' he asked, and raised his hand to swipe at him. Mrs Solade grabbed his hand. ‘Kola please, he's only a child,' she said. For a few moments his parents glared at each other, breathing hard. ‘You see, all of them...bad! Mr. Solade said, and he took his bag and stomped out. ‘Bye-bye,' Jimi muttered under his breath and went back to his room. A few moments later, Jimi stared outside through the window. He saw his parents talking earnestly in front of the house. As his father entered the car, his mother gently touched his cheek. Jimi wondered why.

***

Later that afternoon, Wole came into the room. ‘The old lion has travelled,' Wole said. 'Hip-hip-hooray!' In spite of himself Jimi laughed, but sobered up quickly. ‘Don't let Mum hear you. 'Little bro, you're too serious nowadays. I know you are a genius but you need to lighten up sometimes. Anything bothering you, talk to your big bro. Is it the chicks at school? Let an old pro give you advice. Jimi laughed again. Then he said thoughtfully, "There's this new girl at school; she's really pretty and, you know... 'Ha! Trust my bro,' Wole laughed. And Jimi thought he looked more like his old self-before the bad times. He watched as Wole changed his shirt. ‘Where are you going?' Jimi asked. ‘Nowhere. Jims, can I get some cash?' 'Not till you tell me where you're going. Wole hesitated, 'Okay. You can come with me, but just keep your mouth shut and don't ask any questions.'

It sounded rather ominous, but this was a rare opportunity to spend time with his older brother, especially while he seemed to be in such a good mood. They set off that evening and eventually arrived at a dead end street with several uncompleted buildings. Presently, a man came out of one of the buildings, making furtive gestures with his hands. 'Wait here,' Wole said. He strolled nonchalantly towards the man. The man and Wole spoke for a little while in whispers. There seemed to be a quick exchange-so quick no one would have noticed it-between the man's rapidly moving hands a Wole's. The man gave Wole a thumbs-up and disappeared back into the building. Then Wole walked back to Jimi, stuffing a small nylon bag into his pocket. 'What was that?' Jimi asked. ‘Forget it. Let's go and have some fun." They went to a bar. It was on the ground floor of a block of cramped, evil-smelling apartments. The place was dark and crowded and Nigerian pop music was blasting from the speakers. Wole greeted a group of young men sitting at a table. They were surrounded by bottles of Star and Gulder beer, and Squadron gin. 'Hey yo!' said Wole, giving slapping handshakes all around, 'Who's this?' a rat-faced young man snapped, glaring at Jimi, 'Relax, he's my brother.' Jimi gave them all slapping handshakes too, trying to hide his nervousness. One of them, a man with a street-worn face and short, spiky dreadlocks studied Jimi a moment before declaring, 'Hey-a brother of Wole's is a brother of mine. Drinks!' Jimi wanted to say he didn't drink, then he thought of his father and how angry he would be if he could see him now. He sat down beside a man with bloodshot eyes who was staring vacantly into space and accepted the beer. 'Smoke?' said Rat-face, thrusting out a pack of cigarettes. 'I don't...' Jimi began. Rat-face laughed loudly and Jimi felt embarrassed. Wole half-frowned at him, so he took a cigarette and joined in several rounds of drinks. 'Look at your bro, Wole,' said one of the men. 'He's the man! Just like his brother!' As they drank, Jimi looked around the room and noticed something odd. Half-hidden in the dark corners of the bar. there were women standing with one leg thrust out, as if waiting for someone. Jimi assumed they were waitresses, until one woman saw him staring and fixed him with a sly gaze. He quickly averted his eyes, suddenly realising who they were. The alcohol, the stale smell of cigarette smoke, the strange coded conversation, the dim lighting and the continuous harsh beat of the loud music were starting to dull Jimi's brain. Wole was talking earnestly with the dreadlocked guy, when Rat face jumped up and left the table. When he returned, he brought out a small wrap of rolled paper and lit it. A sharp smell pierced the air. Jimi recognised it. It was a common smell among street boys in bus stops and busy areas in the late evenings. ‘Indian hemp! (Igbo) Suddenly, he felt sick. What was he doing here anyway? He got to his feet a little unsteadily. Wole, I'm going out,' Jimi said, but Wole barely noticed him. He was outside when he saw a black minivan pull up in front of the bar and uniformed figures began jumping out. His heart started to thump. ‘Who's there?' A torch flashed his way. 'Stop!' Jimi didn't wait; he ran. He saw other figures running as well. His heart was beating loudly as he jumped onto the lone rickety bus still plying the road at this late hour and rode it until he got to the stop nearest his home. He was still trembling when he got home. Then he thought about Wole and felt ashamed for running away and leaving his brother like that. Wole came back after midnight. 'Wole!' Jimi jumped on his brother with relief. 'Relax, they found nothing on me. All they wanted was money' He then went to where Jimi's jeans hung and pulled out a packet. ‘What's that! Jimi asked sharply. ‘What's that doing in my pocket?’ ‘Nothing you need to know about.’ Jimi suddenly realised. "You put that stuff in my jeans! What if the police had caught me?' ‘You weren't caught. Jimi wanted to jump on his brother and smash him to pieces. ‘You-you snake!" ‘Cool it, Wole laughed. 'Not unless you want your mam to hear. I'll make it up to you. I promise.' And he walked out. Jimi's head was pounding and he wanted to throw up.

CHAPTER 5

Efua sat writing on her bed. Her aunt had said it was surprising how she had made that room hers so quickly. A little sanctuary. Fresh pink and white sheets on the bed and framed photographs on the table. Everything was always spick and span with the smell of air freshener. She was writing in her diary. Dear diary, It's been years since I've written. I thought I'd outgrown you. I suppose I should be glad I'm here, but nothing can compare to St Catherine's. I can't believe how much I miss everything and everyone, even Hadiza. I'm going to get in touch with Dodo and write a letter of apology to Principal Obange. I'll try to be happy here. It's stupid really, maping and feeling sorry for oneself.

***

Everybody was talking about Efua Coker, the new girl. She was certainly a chick in the boys' eyes, and she was surprisingly bright, doing well in class tests. She hardly ever spoke to anyone and she walked up and down with her nose in the air and a sour expression on her face. The students had already given her a nickname: "The Witch'. 'She thinks she's better than everybody else,' students whispered. "There's nothing special about her, though. Jimi always found himself glancing at her in class. She was gorgeous! If only she'd pay him some attention. Still, he was determined to be friendly. 'Hi,' he said one day after assembly. She didn't answer. 'Hey, it's polite to answer a greeting,' he said. She moved away a little, then turned. 'I believe I know what is polite and not, and I answer who I want to answer to, she said icily, and walked off. Jimi stared after her. People were right. She was nasty! How could she talk to him like that? Did she know who he was? The morning class was taken by Mr. Vann who taught physics. 'Can we cast our minds back to the principle of conservation of linear momentum? What is momentum, by the way?' The class was silent. 'What? You mean to tell me you have no momentum?' he said, smiling at his own joke. 'Solade, can you help us out?' Jimi stood up. He liked moments like this. 'Momentum is the product of a mass of a body and velocity and impulse, and momentum changes as it goes down a slope, he said. 'Very good.' Mr. Vann wrote a problem on the blackboard and handed thc chalk to Jimi. 'Calculate this.' Jimi solved the problem on the blackboard with a flourish and gave the teacher a mock bow. Everyone burst out laughing including dry old Mr. Vann. Only Efua was not laughing. What was so amusing? she wondered. He was just a pompous show off.

***

Jolly was a big boy, an arts student. He liked wearing chains on his trousers and trainers instead of sandals-when he was sure he wouldn't get caught. Efua was standing outside the classroom when he strolled by. He stopped and whistled. 'Hi,' he said and grinned, showing all his teeth. She stared and mumbled something indifferently. 'Yeah, I'm Jolly. Funny name isn't it? You, you're fine! Could we be friends?' She said nothing, hoping he would just go away. He felt a little silly the way she kept staring at him. ‘You look like someone I knew during my, holidays in America but...but she died.' ‘Sorry to hear that. Please excuse me.' ‘Where are you going?' ‘To the guidance counsellor's office. She immediately wished she hadn't said it. ‘I'll walk you.' 'It's not necessary. 'You need guidance, I'll guide you,' he said and he laughed, showing all his teeth again. He kept chattering as they walked. ‘My holidays in the States, I have...' Efua had finally had enough. 'Excuse me, I'd rather walk alone. 'Hey,' he called out and grabbed her hand. She whipped it away. 'Get lost!' she shouted. ‘Excuse me? 'You heard me.' They stared at each other. She was breathing hard and had a harsh expression on her face as she glared at him. Jolly turned away, turned back and turned away again, feeling foolish. ‘I'll deal with you,' he snarled as he walked off.

***

Nene joined Efua after school. 'I heard what happened today between you and Jolly,' she said. 'Did you really tell him to get lost?' Efua sighed. ''He was pestering me. He grabbed my hand.' ‘What did he want? ‘You know, what they all want.' ‘Oh dear. Efua, honey, boys like Jolly-they are mean and can get very unpleasant. ‘I don't want you to become the subject of spiteful gossip and mean tricks. I don't care, Efua said. 'Nene, you're a sweetheart to worry about me, but I'll be fine.' As they moved on, they passed Jimi and Caro talking-or rather Caro was whispering furiously, sounding like a hissing snake. Nene thought Caro was one of the most unpleasant people she had ever known, which was a big thing because she found it difficult to dislike anyone, but Jimi had been nuts about Caro since he was in Class Two. 'There he goes again,' Nene said to herself. Then to Efua she said, 'Jimi also told me you are sort of nasty to him.' She felt duty bound to add, 'You know, Efua, as a Christian-you are a Christian, right?" 'I wish everybody would just leave me alone!' Efua cut her off, frustrated. 'I'm here to mind my own business and read my books.' Nene patted her friend's braids sympathetically. Perhaps, she decided, this wasn't the best time to talk about Jesus to her. 'Jimi, what's the matter?' Caro was saying. 'What do you mean?' 'You know. You've been acting differently, like don't know me.' She narrowed her almond-shaped eyes slightly. 'You've not changed, have you? Remember that girl from the Peter Mary debating team last term?'

'I like that!' Jimi shot back, leaning away from her. 'Remember that university student?' 'Don't change the subject.' Just then, Nene and Efua passed by. Jimi stared at them. Caro followed his eyes. 'Oh, they were right! It's her now, isn't it?' Jimi turned to face her. 'What?' 'You're horrible Jimi! A disgusting, hateful person. You think you're the best thing in the world, don't you? Well, I'll show you.' She stalked off.Jimi stared after her. Girls! Who knew with them? He jogged off to the field. Bayo and some other were already there playing football. He tugged off his shirt people and joined them. ‘What took you so long?' Bayo asked.

'Nothing.' He gave the football such a powerful kick that it went flying high into the sky.

CHAPTER 6

It was drizzling slightly as Nene Ekpo crossed the busy street, she put her hands to her face and listed all her chores for the day she had to pick up her youngest brother from his nursery school, take him home, go to the market to grind pepper in preparation for dinner, and do her school assignments. I'll get round to everything somehow. First things first. The nanny at Mother's Joy Nursery School had a sour expression on her face when Nene arrived. ‘You are late,' she said. ‘I'm sorry, Nene replied. Her brother gave a shout of joy when he saw her and ran towards her. She embraced him tightly. 'Sorry I'm late. I bought you some sweets. Here,' Clutching his hand tightly, they set off. Her parents had a lot of confidence in her. 'Nene is a good girl everybody said. Even her teachers at school and the people at her father's church said so. She came early to school and helped in the children's section in church. She helped her mother clean and tidy the house and care for her younger brother. She could proudly bake delicious cakes and prepare a fine dish of local stews. She had personally given her life to Christ when she was eight years old and church was very important to her. She knew it had kept her from doing a lot of things her schoolmates did. But lately things were changing. Nowadays she found herself staring at the mirror more often. Always a plump, small-eyed girl with short hair bound in thread tied back. Plump neck, plump arms, and plump, slightly bowed legs. Even her chest was plump, which always embarrassed her. She hated the way some of the boys at school glared at it. Of course, it wasn't how one looked that mattered. It was how one was inside. She hated having to remind herself of that. I wish I were pretty. I'm plain Jane. ***

Efua dropped by later that evening while Nene was in the kitchen. ‘Hello Nene,' she stopped. I'm sorry about what I said earlier today. Can I come in? There's no one at my house. You busy? ‘Never mind,' Nene said warmly. 'Come inside. I'm cooking with my mum in the kitchen. Come and join us.' Efua hesitated a little before following Nene to the kitchen. 'Good evening ma. 'Nice to see you, dear, Mrs. Ekpo said over pots of stew on the cooker, which steamed and bubbled. Hope things are going well. Now just help me watch that meat boiling there. That's a good girl. Efua picked up the pot cover gingerly while Nene brought down the plates. 'Your mum's very nice,' Efua told Nene later on after dinner. ‘It's so natural being around her.' 'Your mum must be nice too, Nene ventured. 'Oh yes,' Efua said quickly. "You know she's a businesswoman; busy and all that.' ‘You should meet Jimi's mum, she's very nice too. Maybe if you are nicer to Jimi, you can,' Nene said. You know, he doesn't mean any harm. Even though he's friends with Caro. Nene wondered why she said that last bit. Efua pursed her lips and said nothing, a dark expression on her face. Later that night, as Nene thought it over, she wondered why Efua seemed to dislike Jimi. Actually, it seemed she wasn't particularly interested in being friends with anybody. Nene to do. Caro could be mean sometimes. She often referred wondered why she had mentioned Caro. It wasn't a nice thing to Nene as 'Sister Nene' and had once called her a 'fashion blunder. It occurred to Nene that Caro probably disliked the way Jimi had always been nutty about her. She had been friends with Jimi and Ansa since primary school and she knew everything about them. Ansa, small and thin with his nervous gestures, often confided in her about many things. He seemed so slow, shy and quiet, but boy, could he draw! Perhaps that was why they were close: neither of them was physically attractive, but they were both talented. She was well known in the choir at church and school for possessing lovely soprano voice. Nene was not pretty, but listening to her a sing or speak made people think she was. Jimi was a different matter altogether. Rowdy, but not rough, sometimes thoughtless. He was never unkind. So bright and sporty. She knew all about his troubles with his brother Wole he had always said. and the problems with his parents. 'Nene is my best girlfriend, he had said. During the last year Jimi had changed. He had suddenly grown tall. With his bright, intelligent eyes and dreamy smile, too-except her. all the girls were drawn to him. Jimi was fond of the girls too -except her. Jimi and Efua, there's something fishy going on there, Nene suddenly thought. Efua was by far the prettiest girl in the was always staring at her. senior class. She was already causing some commotion. Jimi was always staring at her. He has never looked at me like that. Nene tried to put away such disturbing thoughts. She was a pastor's daughter and not supposed think about such things. Her door opened suddenly. It was her youngest brother. 'Sister Nene,' he murmured. Please, can you make me some more custard?

CHAPTER 7

About five weeks into the term, the vice principal introduced young woman to the science class. This is Miss Agbenenovi. She is one of the new batch of Youth Corpers serving in Lagos State this year. She will occasionally fill in for Mr. Salami to teach English. The class stared at her in surprise. She was slim and very young looking-not much older than some of the students. Her hair was cut very short and she wore the NYSC uniform of white shirt, a pair of khaki trousers and sand-coloured boots. 'Nice to meet you all. You can call me Miss Novi to make things easier!" she said. The class had to gather in the assembly hall for an impromptu talk about the Mid-Term Dinner. As students trooped out, someone bumped into Efua, making her drop the books she was holding. It was Caro. 'Oh excuse me,' said Efua. 'Excuse you, Caro said coldly and walked off with a group of girls, who giggled as they went. Don't mind her,' a girl beside Efua said, helping her to pick up the books. 'She's a horrible person. It's because of you-know-who.' 'Who?' ‘Jimi Solade. Heard he's sweet on you and she can't stand it. So,' she leaned forward in eager conspiracy, 'is it true?' ‘Of course not,' Efua said with disgust. It was hard enough trying to gain the acceptance of the teachers and pupils here, and having the most popular girl in the school dislike her because of the unwanted attentions of someone called Jimi Solade would not help matters. ‘Juvenile klumps,' she said out loud. 'What?" 'Never mind. Thanks for helping me with my books. I'm Efua ‘I'm Joke. ‘Pleased to meet you.' They went to the hall together. It was already decorated in preparation for the Mid-Term Dinner with banners hanging on the walls and a glass chandelier suspended from the ceiling. A big painting by Ansa was the central focus of the decorations. The school choral group was gathered on stage forming a harmonious chorus together with the beats of the drums. Nene was going to be the singing lead in their cultural dance drama called Oluronbi, based on a folktale. Her trilling voice could be heard above all of them. Babalawo mo wa be be Alu gbin! gbin! Jimi seemed to be everywhere. It suddenly made Efua wish she were doing something as well. ‘Nice painting, she said when she saw Ansa. Ansa stiffened because she had never spoken to him before. He thought he should reply but he couldn't think of anything to say. ‘Jimi came over and said "Hello." 'Um,' she said acidly. 'Have I ever done anything to offend you?" ‘I barely know you." 'Are you going to be at the dinner?' 'What's your business? 'It's a question. This was going badly for Jimi. "Look, why are you so prickly towards me? I'm a nice person. Try me." Good for you,' she snapped and walked off Jimi made a shooting motion after her, and Ansa giggled Jims, she's not human! ‘Of course, Jimi said staring after her. Don't worry, I'll get Suddenly, they heard a loud thump and people were shouting. It was a junior student who had fainted. A group of students gathered around the boy and some pupils were already panicking. ‘Carry him! Pull him! someone cried. ‘Stop! Move aside and give him room for air. It was the new corper. She pushed forward and knelt beside the boy. She felt his neck. They watched her tilt his head upwards a little. Then she opened his mouth wide. ‘Hey, I need assistance,' she told the nearest boy. 'Put your arms straight like this and press his chest there. Press fifteen times and then I'll breathe into his mouth.' They repeated the motions a few times until suddenly the boy spluttered. It was a beautiful moment. ‘Turn him over. Let's carry him quickly to the health centre. I think he has a heart condition. Be very careful and hurry up." The teacher looked gloriously triumphant. Efua stared at her.

***

That Friday was the Mid-Term Dinner, which the students always looked forward to. As Efua and Nene stood in the hall entrance listening to the music pounding within, they both felt awkward. Efua hadn't wanted to come at all, and Nene didn't enjoy dancing. She felt dancing to worldly music was not Christ-like. However, Efua's aunt wouldn't hear of them staying home. ‘School dinners are lovely and you have an opportunity to blend,' she had said. She had even supervised their dressing up. 'Cheer up,' Nene said to Efua. 'You're looking beautiful." Efua was wearing a cream dress and she had dressed her hair so it fell in ringlets in a very attractive fashion. She grimaced and said, 'It's a waste of time. Jimi was part of the organising committee, but his luck wasn't with the ladies recently. The girls left him alone; he was known to belong to Caro whom no one wanted to cross. He caught sight of Efua when they came in. That someone so lovely All the same, thoughts of Caro vanished from his mind. She's a witch, he thought, but what a witch! 'Hey! The DI's voice boomed through the microphone. The party isn't rocking! Grab your partner and feel the beat! Boys stop slacking and girls stop fronting!' Efua and Nene sat down at the table. The first victim came forward. It was Jide, the smallest boy in class. He wore suspenders with his trousers. 'Efua w-w-would you like to dance?' he stammered. 'No,' she said without looking up. He quickly slipped away embarrassed. Efua, that wasn't very nice,' said Nene. 'Too bad.' Dancing soon began in earnest for the impatient students. The teachers stood outside monitoring the event discreetly. If they saw anything too forward, they'd come towards the pair and say, 'We don't allow such things!' Efua kept hoping the time would go by quickly, but the party seemed interminable. She had turned down everybody who asked her to dance; finally, she decided to go to the toilet. But getting there she found a group of students gathered in front of the closed-door giggling and whispering. They straightened up when they saw her. 'No space in there for now!' one called out. She turned back and caught sight of Jolly. He made a rude sign at her, as if to say: You- I'll get you. She felt her blood beginning to boil. Boys! She hated the whole lot of them. When she returned to the party, she saw lide sitting glumly in a corner, looking small and harmless. On an impulse, she turned to him. 'Sorry Jide, I was rather rude earlier. I wasn't in a very good mood, but I'd like to dance with you if you still want to. He looked up uncertainly. She gave him a dazzling smile and held out her hand, leading him to the dance floor. He was shorter than her and he kept stepping on her feet, but she didn't mind. Jimi glared at them both. He couldn't believe it, Efua dancing with Jide of all people. The more he thought about it the angrier he became. Why was she with that pipsqueak? He strolled over to them. ‘Hi,' he said, tapping Jide's shoulder. 'Can you excuse me, please? Come on.' Jide was unwilling to move. Jimi, what are you doing?' Efua asked. 'Stop!' Jimi growled at the smaller boy under his breath. Jide scurried away. ‘What do you mean by that?' Efua said angrily. 'You needed rescuing,' he said. ‘You are a disgusting bully! How dare you!' 'You are a conceited, nasty...' He stopped. 'Look, let's just dance. 'No. I'm leaving! You can dance with yourself!' At that moment the waiter passed by with a tray of drinks. Jimi accidentally bumped into him and the contents of the glasses poured all over Efua. 'You idiot!" she shrieked. Her dress was stained with orange, black and red liquids and froth dripped from her right ear. Jimi wanted the ground to swallow him up and yet, terribly, he wanted to laugh. Efua shrieked again and made for the door in a half run. He moved towards her but she snapped, 'Don't come near me!" She passed Caro who giggled and said, 'You look a mess. That was very unkind of Jimi, and people laughed. Not too many people felt sorry for her. 'Sort of serves her right acting like she's better than everybody…' Outside, a full moon was shining brightly and Efua was wondering how she was going to get home when a voice spoke What is the matter? It was the new teacher, Miss Nov 'Some id…oh. I got drinks spilled on me. 'Oh dear! Why don't we get some water or something?' As they walked, Efua felt suddenly very shy I want to tell you, Miss Novi, that what you did with the boy who fainted was absolutely brilliant She laughed. It's called cardiopulmonary resuscitation. I was a volunteer with an NGO for three months in Sierra Leone.' Efua's eyes opened very wide. Really? Can you tell me all about it? ‘Let's get you cleaned up first.’ It wasn't until much later, after the dance was over and the students were leaving the hall laughing and chattering that Efua stood up. She felt reluctant to end the interesting conversation she was having with Miss Novi. ‘Oh, that was one of the most touching things I ever heard the things you did. There's so much evil in this world! Efua said. ‘You see, I'm interested in such things. Efua continued encouraged by Miss Novi's smile. At my last school I was editor of the magazine and we did some charity work. W called ourselves Angels of Mercy, but it's nothing like what you've done. ‘Ha,' said Miss Novi Angels of Mercy! You do have the face of an angel. Efua ducked her head shyly.

‘Listen, I belong to a group for the support of women's children's rights. ‘Would you like to come along? ‘Would I like it? I would love it! Well then, ‘we'll be seeing you around. I'd better be going. You missed your party!' Miss Novi went off. Just then, Nene ran to meet her. 'Efua, I was looking for you. I'm sorry about what happened. Jimi's very sorry too. What were you doing here?" Talking to the new teacher,' Efua said. She sounded far away. It was nothing really. It doesn't matter.

CHAPTER 8

The term was coming to a close, which meant exams and more excitingly, the Inter-House Sports Tournament. The would be march past rehearsals and football games and race between the four houses: Tiger, Lion, Cheetah and Leopard, every day after classes, pupils gathered at the field to cheer their respective houses. Their voices could be heard chanting in pidgin English We don win o, we don win; Tiger House, Tiger House na you be de one! For Nene, end of term meant organising the Carol Nigh with the music teacher and she was sitting in the cafeteria talking to Efua about it. ‘We don't have enough male voices this year, as usual, Efua, would you like to sing? You have a very nice low voice. You could sing in the tenor section. ‘I can't sing.' 'Please sweetie, for me,' Efua laughed in her unexpectedly rich contralto, I'm afraid I'll be very busy. 'Busy?' ‘Yes. I'm in EGG. It's a group designed for the advancement of women and children. I'm specially involved in a youth programme. Erdoo got me...' 'Who's Erdoo?" 'Miss Novi. ‘You call her Erdoo?' 'Ye-es. I've been going to lots of meetings. We're staging a protest on violence against women. And next week is the empowering youth forum, and we've been visiting the orphanage. Oh, and I've got a Teens Against HIV meeting this evening and for the rest of this week. ‘Gosh Efua, that's really busy, but I'm glad you've found something that interests you." Efua laughed musically again. She is glowing, Nene thought. She looks more beautiful than ever. ‘Don't worry, I'll sing for you, Efua said. She stood up abruptly. 'Excuse me.’ She left just as Jimi came over. He was wearing a sleeveless cotton top and grass stuck to the sides of his legs. ‘Hi Nens, we just won the basketball match. Up Tigers! I just saw the Witch here." ‘Stop calling her that, Nene

said. 'Considering when you were little you tormented her with lizards, and now you're pouring drinks all over her and calling her names, I'm not surprised you two don't get along' ‘Yeah, yeah.
I know she left because of me. She just hates me.' 'Efua's sweet and nice if you get to know her.' 'She can't be like you,' he muttered. 'She went to a girls-only school where things were very different and she's not used to all the gra gra here. ‘What's that?' He wanted to change the subject and pointed at the paper she was holding. ‘The carol list.’ 'Is Efua singing?' 'Yes! ‘Can I join the choir? You're always looking for boys. Nene was astonished. When did Jimi ever sing? Jimi are you sure? You need to have a lot of commitment." 'Don't worry-and I'll help you find some more boys, if you like. Nene stood up, ‘Thanks Jims, I'd appreciate it.' *** The final day of the Inter-House Sports Tournament dawned bright and clear Students wearing the

coloured vests of their respective houses milled about eagerly discussing who would tournament Would it be limi or Icheen? Parents and teachers win the hundred metres race, which was the last event of the sat under shaded tents in the stands. An eager hush settled over the crowd and the eight boys were gathered on the start line, their faces stiff with concentration, Jimi could see Efua in the stands with a slight malicious sneer on her face, as if she could see his fear. A flush of anger rushed through him. Alright, he'd show her! The blast rang out and the boys were off, running like antelopes. From the corner of his eye Jimi could see Icheen. He strained against the air until he felt he was moving against water. Move! Move! They crossed the finish line. ‘Great race for Tiger House!' the microphone boomed. 'Jimi Solade first, Icheen Igbo second...' ‘He won! Nene said smiling. ‘He won,' Efua said unenthusiastically. I'm sure he's feeling like a king now. The posturing peacock who panders to the gallery...' 'Efua, please!' Nene said putting her hands on her ears. 'Not everyone can understand your English.' Joke, who was standing with them, sighed, 'Oh, but he's very nice and dishy too!'

***

The end-of-year Christmas concert took place in the hall, with a large decorated Christmas tree. During the concert Jimi wore a Father Christmas cap on stage, which made everybody laugh, and he sang in the bass section of the choir. He had turned up for every rehearsal. 'Master Solade, you have a very fine baritone, the music teacher had said, delighted. 'Where have you been hiding?" Nene sang all the soprano solos and the group sounded so beautiful that no one could help but be touched. It was a lovely performance, everybody agreed.

The music teacher felt like hugging them all. For Elua, the term had gome very well indeed. The principal had openly commended her on her excellent results and, best of all, she had met Erdon and they were doing things that mattered in the world, like helping the less fortunate, trying to make the world a better place. The only irritating thing had been that Jimi was in the choir. ‘What's up, baby doll? he'd say every day. ‘For the last time, stop calling me baby doll!' ‘Miss Coker, the music teacher always said pettishly, 'can you please pay attention?" Only Ansa was not happy, even though he had designed the murals on stage. He had failed his first term exams and dreaded what his mother would say. Probably: 'No more painting for you, Ansa. How many times must I tell you...? Jimi camc to takc a bow onc last time. He had won the best athlete's trophy and a prize for the best exam results again, and all the girls were cooing at him. The handsome schoolboy spread his arms wide and smiled. Everybody loves Jimi, the whole school seemed to be saying to him.

CHAPTER 9

Whenever people said clichés like the darkest part of the night just before down, they were usually right, but could they also mean that the brightest days occurred before the darkest nights? It was something Jimi Solade would think about for many years afterwards. Those days of being a schoolboy in Forcados were bright: he won prizes, he was popular, and the only bad thing was that Efua Coker didn't like him. He didn't spend much time thinking about his family, then Mother was quiet and gentle and always made sure he had good food to eat and that his clothes were clean and ironed. Father grumbled incessantly and Wole...was simply Wole. He was now doing some sort of computer diploma course at an institute, although he kept trying to see if their elder brother, Femi, who was living in the United Kingdom, would help him travel out or at least send some money to him.

Femi was just like Mr. Solade: he wanted nothing to do with Wole. Throughout the holidays, Jimi went out to parties with all his friends and had a good time at the beach. Once they went to a nightclub for the fun of it; nobody guessed they were under-age. One night, just after New Year's Day when his father was away for his job and Wole was not at home, Jimi heard a pounding on his bedroom door. It was Risikat, the househelp. 'Mummy has fainted,' she said with terror in her eyes. She was just standing there, then she moved back and fell. Help us!' He ran to the kitchen and saw his mother on the ground. One of her arms was flung wide and she had a little cut on her forehead where she had hit the cupboard. He suddenly realised how thin she was. 'Mum, mum can you hear me?' There was no answer. Risikat was staring at him, rolling her frightened eyes. For a second he didn't know what to do; he suddenly felt sick, as if he was going to faint as well. Pulling himself together, he bent close and felt her slight breath against his face. She was still alive. Thank God! Jimi took a wet cloth from the househelp and rubbed his mother's forehead, his heart racing. After about five minutes, Mrs. Solade woke up and Jimi and the house help helped her to the sitting room. 'Mum, are you okay? What's the matter?' Jimi asked. ‘I'm alright,' she said weakly. 'No Mum, you're not. Have you been ill?' There was something about the way she refused to meet his gaze that made him uncomfortable. Jimi pressed until she finally agreed to go to the hospital for a check-up. There, the doctor spent a long time with her. 'We'll have to admit her,' he said when he finally came out of the examination room, 'just for some tests.

***

After an agonising night, Jimi went back to the hospital the next day to find his mother sitting up in bed. The ward she was in had two other beds in it, one of which was occupied by an elderly woman who lay still, occasionally punctuating the air with noisy gasping breaths. Jimi wasn't sure if she was conscious or not. Jimi twisted his nostrils a little at the peculiar antiseptic smell that hospitals always seemed to have. 'Are you feeling better, Mummy?' 'Jimi,' she said, 'I want to tell you something." His heart stood still. Yet, she said nothing. 'Mum, tell me. I'm not a child. 'I have cancer. Ovarian cancer? His throat went dry as he struggled to understand what she had just said. "The that sounds bad. His voice trailed off Cancer! It meant people who became painfully thin with. hopeless looking eyes and bald heads. It was something that happened to other people, something that one read about in books or watched on television. How long had she known What was going to happen now? It seemed suddenly darker inside the ward. The smells around him grew thicker he wanted to throw up. He glanced at the yellow eyed woman on the other bed breathing heavily with her bluish tongue hanging out. The world was suddenly full of sickness and ugliness. There was silence and then she said something he did not expect. 'Your father, he loves you both! Why did she say that? He wondered. 'Dad?' ‘Yes. He can't help the way he gets angry sometimes. He almost went bankrupt after what your brother did. I'm going to try and pull through this and look after you all. I don't want you to worry about me! "Worry?" He sat on the bed and he suddenly felt like crying. Tears filled his eyes in spite of himself. He hoped this was a bad dream. ‘Don't worry,' she kept saying. I'll get through this. Don't worry at all. *** Mr. Solade came back from his trip the next day looking confused. Jimi had called him at once, early the day before Uncle Kazeem was also around. "What's happened?' he growled at Jimi when he arrived at the house. 'She's really ill said Jimi. His father looked stunned, then recovered himself ‘Where is that good for nothing brother of yours? ‘He was around,' Jimi said guardedly. Wole had arrived at the hospital the day before. He had hung around for a short while muttering, 'I hate hospitals,' before disappearing again They drove in silence to the hospital and Mr. Solade spoke to the doctors. His mother kept asking him how things were going at home and how Wale was. One would think she was not the sick one. After a while, Mr. Solade said to Jimi, 'Let's go.’ ‘I'm not going yet.' ‘Don't start with me. I'm not going, Papa! Please leave me alone, Jimi shouted. They gazed at each other. For the first time Jimi understood how it felt to be like Wole and defy his father. An old fear of his father tugged at the back of his mind, but he was past caring. Jimi, obey your father, Mrs. Solade said, 'Please'. On the way to the car his father said, 'From now on I'll keep an eye on you and that good-for-nothing brother of yours. Both of you will have to deal with me.' Then he muttered something unintelligible. Later in the evening, Wole came back and received a furious tongue lashing, but that was all, Afterwards, he came to see Jimi, looking sorry for once. 'How's she doing?" Wole asked. 'She's better than she was,' Wole twisted his hands in his pockets. 'Damn, I feel so bad. Has she really got...you know?' 'Yes,' Jimi's voice was bitter.

'I never even noticed anything.' 'None of us noticed,' When Ansa heard that Mrs. Solade was ill, he and his parents came to visit Mrs. Solade in the hospital. He sat with Jimi on a bench outside the ward. Nene joined them. She and her parents had also come to offer their support. ‘I hope she gets better soon,' Ansa said. ‘I'll be praying for her and all of you,' Nene said and gave him a hug. 'She'll get better, Jimi. Just have faith.' 'Yes, she will.' Jimi's heart was heavy as he said it. Chapter Ten Second term had started. The chemistry laboratory was filled with serious faced students. One held up a test tube filled with a green liquid. "Bingo!" he said. Jims, this would indicate ferrous iron wouldn't it?" 'Um...it should.' Jimi replied absently. Mr. Edet, the chemistry teacher came to their table 'How are you all doing?' ‘Just fine sir,' they chorused. ‘Solade, you wait behind after lab.' Jimi murmured a little. He looked round and saw Efua filling a burette, eyebrows puckered in concentration. She looked up, their eyes met and she quickly glanced away. He wondered why she had been staring. After classes Mr. Edet asked Jimi to help tidy up in the laboratory. He led the way into the back room that was usually empty, but was now filled with microscopes, burettes and other new equipment. 'Brand new stuff for your exams,' said Mr. Edet, rubbing hishands. 'You students don't know how lucky you are.' 'It's good, sir,' Jimi said politely. Mr. Edet stopped and peered at him short sightedly. 'Is anything wrong?" ‘N-nothing sir.' 'Good to hear that.' He patted Jimi's head paternally. "You can join the technician-help him preserve and labcl thc snake. Give him the key to the cupboard where the formalin is kept. It's on that cabinet. ‘Thank you, sir, but I think I should be getting home now." It was well past four and the grounds were empty. He leaned against a wall and thought of his last visit to the hospital and the silent drip-drip of the intravenous chemotherapy line draining into his mother's arm. She was in so much pain these days sometimes her eyes seemed to say, 'I want this to end…’ He bent over and vomited onto the grass. Then he went to the tap and washed his mouth and hands. Efua came upon Jimi as he was wiping his hand with a handkerchief. She had stayed behind too, helping Miss Novi plan a weekend campaign against child hawking. ‘Do be careful, Miss Novi had said just before leaving. I heard there was a clash between some area boys this morning around here' ‘I didn't hear anything like that, Efua had said. Anyway, don't worry. The teacher had patted her cheek lightly and for a minute they'd gazed at each other affectionately. As Efua walked along, the air seemed sweeter and colours brighter. Until she saw Jimi. ‘Oh,' she said. ‘Oh... he mumbled. She had always thought Jimi was cocky and irritating but today there seemed something helpless about him and, in spite of herself, she felt a tenderness for him-like the tenderness she felt for helpless creatures, like baby birds. Why, she suddenly thought, he looks just like a child really. A poor little kid. He stood up straight. 'Excuse me.' Wait,' she said. 'I don't mean to pry, but Nene said your mum wasn't feeling too well. I hope she's better now.' ‘Thanks, he answered shortly. They stood staring at each other a little awkwardly. Then he said, I'm going home, are you?" And that was how they found themselves walking together towards the school gate. Efua was already regretting her impulse. She didn't like walking with boys Hope he doesn't start any nonsense again, she thought. Meanwhile, Jimi was trying hard not to glance at her. She booked fresh and you and fastidiously neat, as always. Her gentle perfume filled the air. Her boobies were...shame on you, Jimi, he thought, catching himself. Your mother is in hospital and you’re having thoughts like that! They turned down the street and she started to say something when they heard gunshots. Suddenly the noise of people screaming and glass breaking filled the air. 'What's that? Erua gripped Jimi's hand in fear. People were running helter skelter and a tray of oranges rolled in the dust. The young girl hawking them was wailing loudly, but nobody paid any attention to her. 'Area boys and the police are fighting, someone shouted. If you love yourself stay out of the way!' Jimi and Efua joined a group and ran towards an uncompleted building. 'We'd best stay here, Jimi said when they got inside. He noticed almost regretfully that Efua had released his hand. More people filled the street shouting and adding to the commotion, when Efua said, 'I know that boy!' 'Who?' Jimi asked. He saw she was pointing at a plump boy of about ten years old who stood in the middle of the street staring blankly. He had small, squinty eyes and an oddly shaped head that seemed too large for his body. 'Is he from the school for retarded children? 'Children with learning disabilities; she corrected him primly and then said with alarm, 'He's going to get hurt.' She was moving forward. 'Don't tell me you're going there. You can't!" Jimi called. She looked at him in astonishment. ‘And who will stop me?' She ran out and, cursing under his breath, Jimi followed her. The air was filled with blinding smoke that stung their eyes. A policeman was beating a man lying on the ground with the butt of his rifle. When the man raised his head, they saw it was covered with blood. Efua grabbed the boy's hand and then someone pushed her from behind. She reeled forward, almost falling into the nearby gutter, but Jimi caught her. 'Run! he shouted, and they ran out of the smoke, pulling the boy along with them. They kept running until they were far from the heat and noise of the unrest. She was trembling and Jimi had a small cut on his lip. The boy burst into tears. ‘Look,’ Jimi said, 'if we stay here the trouble can come here. I know the owner of that ice cream bar. It's not totally shut yet. ‘He'll let us in.' ‘Lucky for us,' she gasped. They banged on the burglar bars and a man peered through the glass apprehensively. Samu, the owner, was a family friend of Jimi's. His expression changed when he saw them and he opened the bars. The place was air-conditioned and had a television. Jimi The Great! How are you? Always trouble in this Lagos,' he said. Then he lowered his voice, 'And who's this one now? It's not Caro and it's not Dupe or...’ 'Stop it.' Jimi almost blushed. 'She's just my classmate.' ‘That's why you are looking so sheepish. I don't blame you, though; she's a wow.' Efua was seated with the boy, her arm round his shoulders. ‘I'm sorry,' she said. 'You like doing crazy things. Crazy nice things.' Jimi grinned. She undid the band tying her hair. She hadn't plaited it this week and it was long and thick and fell across her shoulders. 'I don't. Bad things just always happen when you're around. I'll take that as a joke!' ‘They both laughed and she said, 'It was terrible, but you were nice,' almost reluctantly. ‘Yes, I am nice. How did you get involved with him? Jimi pointed to the boy lovely ‘Through a charity visit I once helped with. It was lovely and I learned a lot about children like him and the way society sees them," she said in a serious voice. It sounded rather silly to Jimi, but the talk went on to things like safety on the streets, school life, pcople, places and so on. Once or twice they laughed. Jimi had never heard her laugh before this. The boy also cheered up considerably, pointing at things and staring at the television. Samu brought them free ice cream and winked at Jimi. ‘Why did you leave your other school? Jimi asked. ‘I wanted to leave, now I regret it. "Oh!?' ‘I'll tell you more about that another time, not now." By the time the unrest finally died down, it was dark. ‘I think we should be going now. My aunt will be worried. Efua said. There's no one at home to worry about me, Jimi suddenly thought and he felt downcast. 'We have to drop him off," she said pointing at the little boy. After thanking Samu, they took the boy to his boarding school. 'Bless you both,' the instructor said when they arrived with the child. "You are wonderful children? On their way home they chatted and laughed. The streets seemed magically changed -like her. Coloured lights flashed from billboards with words like: NAIJA 4 LIFE! WETIN DEY! Traders selling piles of oranges sat talking as paraffin lamps glowed like magic candles on their trays. Cheerful music sounded from shops and restaurants. A man with dreadlocks leaned against a wall and played a guitar softly as they passed the park. Just opposite, a white garment church service was in full swing with noisy, chanting prayers and stamping feet. A girl selling recharge cards beside her stall danced to the music of popular pop star Burna Boy, which was playing from a nearby shop. She shook, twisted and bent with such reckless abandon that Jimi and Efua stopped and laughed as well, infected with pure fun. Except for the broken glass on the ground, it seemed impossible that there had been trouble just that afternoon. ‘They stopped in front of her house. "Thanks for today,' she said, smiling at him. "You were, you know...' she stopped as if she had said too much, smiled at him and squeezed his hand a little Jimi realised they had been holding hands the whole time. 'Goodnight.' And she went inside. Jimi continued towards his house. The day seemed to have lasted forever. The sky was full of twinkling stars and there was a full moon. He bounced along, sometimes jumping, sometimes breaking into a run. A few people stared at him, wondering what this boy in a school uniform jacket was all about.

When he went to sleep that night there was a half-smile on his face.

CHAPTER 10

Second term had started. The chemistry laboratory was filled with serious faced students. One held up a test tube filled with a green liquid. "Bingo!" he said. Jims, this would indicate ferrous iron wouldn't it?" 'Um...it should.' Jimi replied absently. Mr. Edet, the chemistry teacher came to their table 'How are you all doing?' ‘Just fine sir,' they chorused. ‘Solade, you wait behind after lab.’ Jimi murmured a little. He looked round and saw Efua filling a burette, eyebrows puckered in concentration. She looked up, their eyes met and she quickly glanced away. He wondered why she had been staring. After classes Mr. Edet asked Jimi to help tidy up in the laboratory. He led the way into the back room that was usually empty, but was now filled with microscopes, burettes and other new equipment. 'Brand new stuff for your exams,' said Mr. Edet, rubbing hishands. 'You students don't know how lucky you are.' 'It's good, sir,' Jimi said politely. Mr. Edet stopped and peered at him short-sightedly. 'Is anything wrong?" ‘N-nothing sir.' 'Good to hear that.' He patted Jimi's head paternally. "You can join the technician-help him preserve and label the snake. Give him the key to the cupboard where the formalin is kept. It's on that cabinet. ‘Thank you, sir, but I think I should be getting home now." It was well past four and the grounds were empty. He leaned against a wall and thought of his last visit to the hospital and the silent drip-drip of the intravenous chemotherapy line draining into his mother's arm. She was in so much pain these days sometimes her eyes seemed to say, 'I want this to end…' He bent over and vomited onto the grass. Then he went to the tap and washed his mouth and hands. Efua came upon Jimi as he was wiping his hand with a handkerchief. She had stayed behind too, helping Miss Novi plan a weekend campaign against child hawking. ‘Do be careful, Miss Novi had said just before leaving. I heard there was a clash between some area boys this morning around here' ‘I didn't hear anything like that, Efua had said. Anyway, don't worry. The teacher had patted her cheek lightly and for a minute they'd gazed at each other affectionately. As Efua walked along, the air seemed sweeter and colours brighter. Until she saw Jimi. ‘Oh,' she said. ‘Oh... he mumbled. She had always thought Jimi was cocky and irritating but today there seemed something helpless about him and, in spite of herself, she felt a tenderness for him-like the tenderness she felt for helpless creatures, like baby birds. Why, she suddenly thought, he looks just like a child really. A poor little kid. He stood up straight. 'Excuse me.' Wait,' she said. 'I don't mean to pry, but Nene said your mum wasn't feeling too well. I hope she's better now.' ‘Thanks, he answered shortly. They stood staring at each other a little awkwardly. Then he said, I'm going home, are you?" And that was how they found themselves walking together towards the school gate. Efua was already regretting her impulse. She didn't like walking with boys Hope he doesn't start any nonsense again, she thought. Meanwhile, Jimi was trying hard not to glance at her. She booked fresh and you and fastidiously neat, as always. Her gentle perfume filled the air. Her boobies were...shame on you, Jimi, he thought, catching himself. Your mother is in hospital and you're having thoughts like that! They turned down the street and she started to say something when they heard gunshots. Suddenly the noise of people screaming and glass breaking filled the air. 'What's that? Erua gripped Jimi's hand in fear. People were running helter skelter and a tray of oranges rolled in the dust. The young girl hawking them was wailing loudly, but nobody paid any attention to her. ‘Area boys and the police are fighting, someone shouted. If you love yourself stay out of the way!' Jimi and Efua joined a group and ran towards an uncompleted building. ‘We'd best stay here, Jimi said when they got inside. He noticed almost regretfully that Efua had released his hand. More people filled the street shouting and adding to the commotion, when Efua said, 'I know that boy!' ‘Who?' Jimi asked. He saw she was pointing at a plump boy of about ten years old who stood in the middle of the street staring blankly. He had small, squinty eyes and an oddly shaped head that seemed too large for his body. 'Is he from the school for retarded children? ‘Children with learning disabilities; she corrected him primly and then said with alarm, 'He's going to get hurt.' She was moving forward. 'Don't tell me you're going there. You can't!" Jimi called. She looked at him in astonishment. ‘And who will stop me?' She ran out and, cursing under his breath, Jimi followed her. The air was filled with blinding smoke that stung their eyes. A policeman was beating a man lying on the ground with the butt of his rifle. When the man raised his head, they saw it was covered with blood. Efua grabbed the boy's hand and then someone pushed her from behind. She reeled forward, almost falling into the nearby gutter, but Jimi caught her. 'Run! he shouted, and they ran out of the smoke, pulling the boy along with them. They kept running until they were far from the heat and noise of the unrest. She was trembling and Jimi had a small cut on his lip. The boy burst into tears. ‘Look,’ Jimi said, 'if we stay here the trouble can come here. I know the owner of that ice cream bar. It's not totally shut yet. ‘He'll let us in.' ‘Lucky for us,' she gasped. They banged on the burglar bars and a man peered through the glass apprehensively.

Samu, the owner, was a family friend of Jimi's. His expression changed when he saw them and he opened the bars. The place was air-conditioned and had a television. Jimi The Great! How are you? Always trouble in this Lagos,' he said. Then he lowered his voice, 'And who's this one now? It's not Caro and it's not Dupe or...' 'Stop it.' Jimi almost blushed. 'She's just my classmate.' 'That's why you are looking so sheepish. I don't blame you, though; she's a wow.' Efua was seated with the boy, her arm round his shoulders. 'I'm sorry,' she said. 'You like doing crazy things. Crazy nice things.' Jimi grinned. She undid the band tying her hair. She hadn't plaited it this week and it was long and thick and fell across her shoulders. 'I don't. Bad things just always happen when you're around. I'll take that as a joke!' 'They both laughed and she said, 'It was terrible, but you were nice,' almost reluctantly. 'Yes, I am nice. How did you get involved with him? Jimi pointed to the boy lovely 'Through a charity visit I once helped with. It was lovely and I learned a lot about children like him and the way society sees them," she said in a serious voice. It sounded rather silly to Jimi, but the talk went on to things like safety on the streets, school life, people, places and so on. Once or twice they laughed. Jimi had never heard her laugh before this. The boy also cheered up considerably, pointing at things and staring at the television. Samu brought them free ice cream and winked at Jimi. 'Why did you leave your other school? Jimi asked. 'I wanted to leave, now I regret it. "Oh!?' 'I'll tell you more about that another time, not now." By the time the unrest finally died down, it was dark. 'I think we should be going now. My aunt will be worried. Efua said. There's no one at home to worry about me, Jimi suddenly thought and he felt downcast. 'We have to drop him off," she said pointing at the little boy.

After thanking Samu, they took the boy to his boarding school. 'Bless you both,' the instructor said when they arrived with the child. "You are wonderful children? On their way home they chatted and laughed. The streets seemed magically changed -like her. Coloured lights flashed from billboards with words like: *NAIJA 4 LIFE!*

WETIN DEY! Traders selling piles of oranges sat talking as paraffin lamps glowed like magic candles on their trays. Cheerful music sounded from shops and restaurants. A man with dreadlocks leaned against a wall and played a guitar softly as they passed the park. Just opposite, a white garment church service was in full swing with noisy, chanting prayers and stamping feet. A girl selling recharge cards beside her stall danced to the music of popular pop star Burna Boy, which was playing from a nearby shop. She shook, twisted and bent with such reckless abandon that Jimi and Efua stopped and laughed as well, infected with pure fun. Except for the broken glass on the ground, it seemed impossible that there had been trouble just that afternoon. ‘They stopped in front of her house. "Thanks for today,' she said, smiling at him. "You were, you know...' she stopped as if she had said too much, smiled at him and squeezed his hand a little Jimi realised they had been holding hands the whole time. 'Goodnight.' And she went inside. Jimi continued towards his house. The day seemed to have lasted forever. The sky was full of twinkling stars and there was a full moon. He bounced along, sometimes jumping, sometimes breaking into a run. A few people stared at him, wondering what this boy in a school uniform jacket was all about. When he went to sleep that night there was a half-smile on his face.

CHAPTER 11

'Jimi, you've been missing football practice.' Bayo, limi's friend, asked, "What's wrong?" 'I've been busy. 'Okay. Hope you're coming for CK's bash tonight. 'Oh, I'd forgotten. Don't think I'll be there. 'Come on, when did you ever miss a party? It'll be great. There will be snooker and all the girls will be there.' Jimi hesitated and said, 'Bayo, don't you think there's more to life than just partying? Anyway, I want to study. Bayo looked at him in mock horror. You of all people! You never need to study and you always come out tops. About then Efua and Nene passed, smiling and saying hello as they walked by. Since the day of the disturbances, he and Efua had become friendlier. Sometimes, the four of them- he, Ansa, Nene and Efua-went to the hospital together, and Nene always said a short prayer. It always made him feel much better. 'Jimi Striker! When did you and the Witch start saying hello? Bayo laughed. 'She's not that bad really. 'Oh well, if you say so. See you at practice.' Jimi arrived for practice late. 'Solade, what's the matter with you?' The football coach snarled. 'I'm sorry sir," he said lamely. 'We have important matches coming up. I could kick you out of the team. 'I...' 'Shut up. Get on the field! During practice he kept missing passes. Jims, what's wrong with you?' a teammate yelled in frustration. 'Don't know,' he said, equally frustrated. 'Solade, you are playing like a legless cockroach!" the coach shouted from the sidelines. 'Don't mind him, he's been going home to eat mama's food, another teammate said innocently. This was too much. Jimi pounced on the boy and they rolled on the pitch, kicking and punching. The others had to drag him away. 'Solade, get out of here! Frog jump out!' shouted the coach. Jimi looked at the shocked faces of his teammates. He knew they were all wondering about his erratic behaviour, and he wanted to say he was sorry. Instead, he ran off.

***

Mrs. Solade died on a Saturday morning. It had rained heavily the night before and on his way to the hospital the city gutters were gurgling ominously. He was with her when she stopped breathing. He shouted for the doctor and nurse and they rushed in and pushed him out. Later, the doctor explained to his father that they had done their best, but that the prognosis was very poor. His father put an arm around Jimi's shoulders and said, 'We understand.' ''We are very sorry,' said the doctor. Jimi was quiet, but it seemed as if he was watching everything from a distance. Someone was shouting 'Mummy! Mummy! Jimi wasn't sure if it was him.

***

Their apartment had been full of visitors since then. Uncle Kazeem, Aunt Memunat, Aunty Omotunde and a host of other relatives that Jimi half knew. Their oldest brother Femi arrived from the UK. He was smaller than Jimi remembered and he enfolded him in a bear hug. Femi had never done that before. Usually, he was dealing out blows for the slightest thing Once, when Jimi was small. Femi flung him down staircase-by accident, he claimed. Father had given Femi the beating of his life then. Now, Femi sat in his expensive clothe and said, 'I can't believe this. Wole wandered in and out like a ghost. Jimi kept expecting his mother to come in and say something like, 'Imagine them saying I was dead! What would you like to eat?' it would never happen. She was buried in a private cemetery and some of his school friends attended the funeral. The coffin made scraping sounds as it was lowered into the grave and he couldn't see through the tears that blinded him. He moved off to a deserted part of the cemetery, wishing and praying it was all a bad dream and he would wake up. ‘Please, God... he choked. What could he say? He sank down to the ground. He heard footsteps beside him. It was Efua. ‘I’m...sorry,' she said. She stood for a little while, then sat down beside him. ‘I don't know...I'm-I'm not close to my mother, but I can see how much you loved yours, and she went silent. He clasped his hand over hers. She tightened her fingers over his and they sat quietly for what seemed like a long time. until Nene and Ansa came over. 'Your dad is looking for you,' Ansa said to Jimi. Efua jumped up when she heard his voice and stared at her hands. "Thanks," Jimi said, and went back to his family.

CHAPTER 12

Shortly afterwards, Mr. Solade told his sons he was travelling out of the country. He said he was about to secure an important financial deal and might be away for as long as five months. 'Five months!" Jimi gasped. 'Yes, I promise you boys will be fine. I'll leave plenty of money for you and I'll send you more regularly. Money, money. That was all Jimi's father thought about. 'Listen, Mr. Solade said to Jimi, almost gruffly, I'm proud of and I know you can look after that brother of yours. I'm for future education and give you boys trying to save up your the best. Things have been tough recently. My dear wife now resting in heaven understood that.' What about me? Jimi wanted to shout. Responsible younger brother indeed. At that moment Jimi almost hated him. When he left, both brothers saw him off at the airport. Jimi never thought he could miss his father, but as Mr. Solade went through the departures gate, Jimi suddenly had the terrifying feeling he might never come back. 'Chin up, bro,' Wole said when they got back home, but Jimi slumped on the bed. 'Both our parents are gone now,' said Jimi. Wole brought out a wrap. 'I have something for you. A nice smoke. Are you in?' 'What's that?" 'Come on, let's light up and take it. All our worries will soon go.' 'I... I don't know...' 'Come on, just this once I have your back. I'm your bro, not so? –

***

Wole went wild Every day, questionable visitors trooped and out of the apartment and every weekend was a party. He ran through his money like water. 'The noise from that flat is just too much, Mr. Izaegbegbe Ansa's father, grumbled to his wife one morning. 'Poor boys, Ansa's mother said. "That is what comes out leaving your children all alone. That day, she made it a point to visit the boys. ‘Is everything all right?" she asked Jimi when she arrived. ‘Yes, Ma ‘Listen darling, if you need anything or you're worried about anything just come and see me." After she left, Jimi tried to talk to his brother. ‘Wole, we can't allow those guys in here anymore." ‘Why not? It's my house as much as yours." ‘It's too much. They mess up the whole place." ‘You sound just like the old man. Relax and take life easy, bro.’ Jimi looked around Wole's room. There was some brownish white powder on a sheet of paper. ‘What's that? Wole suddenly laughed. It was an ugly laugh. You don't want to know Jimi remembered smoking the wrap the day their father left and the light-headed feeling he got afterwards. He'd said he would never try it again. There was something in him that always wanted to try things, to take a dare. ‘I'm not a kid' ‘You want something different? Alright, fine by me. Wole closed the door. Jimi's heart beat loudly but he moved forward. ‘Remove your watch and roll up your sleeves. This will be the ultimate experience. Heroin.’ Heroin. Once a psychologist had come to school to give a talk on the dangers of drug use. She had mentioned heroin. ‘One of the worst drugs out there, the woman had said. She showed them a short film of a scrawny white man writhing and gasping in the throes of heroin withdrawal. These things happened in other countries, not in Jimi Solade's room, not with his own brother. Maybe there was something in those drugs that could make him forget reality. It was a tempting thought. An image of his mother's face floated into his head. She was alive and glowing. ‘No, Wole, he whispered. Wole shrugged and laughed. 'I didn't think so, he said smugly and left the room. How low he has sunk, Jimi thought. Wole was lost. He began to sob hard, bitter tears.

***

Jimi was feeling sick. Throughout class he felt sleepy. Afterwards, the math's teacher spoke to him, 'Jimi, you scored disgracefully low in the last test. This has never happened before, what's wrong?' Jimi mumbled, I'm sorry' It was difficult to think with his brain feeling woolly. He just wanted to get through the day. Who could he talk to about Wole? They'd all run to the police and he didn't want to snitch on his brother. Besides, Wole had never mentioned the drugs again. In fact, he had stopped talking to Jimi altogether. Nene and Efua cornered Jimi after class. 'Jimi, are you alright?' Efua asked. She was staring at him intently. 'Fine,' he said abruptly and he quickly moved off. The way she looked at him made him uncomfortable. The girls stopped to talk to Ansa after school. 'Don't you two think Jimi's been looking odd these last couple of days?' Efua asked as they all walked home together. 'Yes,' Nene said. 'Have you tried finding out what's wrong?' 'No. Maybe he's not feeling well. 'I'm worried too,' Ansa said. 'Why?' Efua said sharply. Ansa hesitated before speaking. 'He's staying alone with his brother. 'What about his brother?" Ansa licked his lips and said furtively, 'Look, this is between you and me. Jimi would be very angry if I told but his brother is-well, we suspect he sometimes sells drugs and…' Ansa didn't complete the sentence. Nene gasped, but Efua said angrily, 'What a brother!' 'Of course Jimi would never indulge in anything like that, but he's very keen on his brother and I know he's worried. Jimi needs help,' Efua said. 'Maybe you can talk to him,' Ansa said. 'Me?' Efua cocked her head and Nene looked away. 'We can go there tonight-it's Friday-and just talk to him.

***

When they got to the Solades' apartment that evening, the door was open, the lights were dim and loud music was blaring from an unseen stereo. There were people lounging about and dancing. The three friends stood for a minute watching everyone. 'I'm not sure about this,' Nene said. 'Don't worry, it will be all right,' said Efua, straining her eyes. Where is he?' A boy came over. 'Hey, baby. Care for a dance?' he asked Efua. 'We're looking for Jimi Solade,' Efua said firmly. He pointed. 'Just over there, sitting on the armchair. He looks finished,' he laughed. They picked their way towards him. 'Wake up!' Ansa said, shaking him. Jimi opened his eyes and leapt to his feet, looking around flustered and confused. 'Nene. Efua. What are you? 'You seem to be having a nice time, Nene said. 'Oh we… He rubbed his neck. 'Let's all go outside, Efua suggested.

Outside, Nene started delicately. ‘Jims, we’ve been worried about you.” He tried to smile. “There’s nothing wrong. Want to join the ‘What party? Lying on a chair looking miserable? Efua snapped. ‘Hey, Jimi flared. What do you know about me?’ Nene quickly interrupted. ‘Jimi, we want to tell you something Please stop all this. We need you and we’re all missing you. You can’t stay here without being corrupted further. This isn’t you.’ ‘You can stay with mc, Ansa said. ‘My mother would love to have you around.” Jimi stared at all of them ‘I…I-‘ ‘Please, Efua said softly and moved closer, her eyes bright. ‘Do it. Please. He felt his knees going weak. ‘Oh…yes. Ok. I will… What an angel! Jimi thought.

***

Later that night, as Nene and Efua walked home, Nene spoke up. ‘You seemed very concerned about Jimi.' ‘He's in a really bad way and he's all alone.'

‘Listen Efua, I know you like doing lots of good works but... Her voice trailed away as if she was embarrassed. "What?" 'Remember Jimi is a human being, not one of your causes. Efua stopped. "That's an unfair thing to say ‘It wouldn't be fair to him if you're just saying these things because you're feeling sorry for him.' ‘Thank you very much, Efua said coldly, and walked off.

CHAPTER 13

Two weeks later, the Forcados football team was playing. friendly match against the nearby St Edmund's Comprehensive School and most of the students were gathered cheer their team Drums and yells followed every pass and dribble. Even though he wasn't playing, Jimi stood on the lines with a red bandana tied around his head to support his fellow teammates. To everybody's relief, he was more himself these days. ‘He's getting over his mum's death, people said. At half time, he raced over to where Efua stood. ‘Glad you're now a football fan, he said. I wish I was playing!’ She laughed. Efua wanted to buy a drink and Jimi wet with her. Nene watched them go. She and Efua had been rather cool with each other since their little tiff. As soon as they were gone, Nene heard a voice sneer, 'Mickey and Minnie Mouse! She acted as if she couldn't stand the sight of him!’ it was Caro, she had been watching them too and her face was a vicious mask. Nene moved away from the other girl and bumped into Ansa, who was holding a large square of canvas. ‘Hey Nens,' Ansa greeted her. 'Glad to see Jimi's out of his slump. ‘Is he okay staying with you?' ‘Yeah. He's with us most nights and he studies. He's helping me too. ‘Nice to hear that.' She took the canvas. ‘You're painting again. She looked at the painting closely. ‘It's Efua!' she exclaimed in surprise. ‘Don't tell her yet,' Ansa said shyly, 'I used to think she was a mean person until...but she's told me she likes my paintings and she encourages me.' Nene said nothing as she returned the painting to Ansa. *** At the food kiosk, Jimi and Efua fell to talking. ‘You know what,' Efua said, 'I want to be a doctor, because I think it would be nice to help people. I think I can do it. What do you think?' ‘You'll be a drop dead gorgeous doctor,' he said. ‘Is that all there is?' she said somewhat sadly. Why won't stop thinking about how I look? she thought. ‘I know you can do it. Me? I don't think I could ever be a doctor.' ‘Why not? You're smart enough.' Jimi remembered his mother in hospital. Fat lot of good the doctors did, he thought bitterly. 'How's your brother doing? I know you don't like talking about it. It was strange how people changed when you saw them differently, Jimi realised. At that moment some voices floated from over thc wall saying, You can touch the sky 'Cause you're so fly My love's so high... It's the Rhymers,' Jimi laughed. Their flow seems to be going strong today. 'Silly lyrics,' she said, but she laughed too.

***

That afternoon, Nene headed to Efua's house. She hated holding grudges, so she had decided she would go and collect her biology textbook from

Efua and reconcile with her. Efua was not at home-she wasn't back from the football match yet-but her aunt allowed her to get the book from her room. Mrs. Alli hesitated a little and then said, 'Nene, Efuas worrying me.' ‘Efua, why? ‘She's so busy with all her activities, going here and there It's good, but she takes it so seriously. She's not Mother Teresa.’ Nene smiled. I don't think it's anything to worry about: ‘And she's so close with that new teacher, Efua's aunt murmured. ‘Elua's doing very well at school, Ma,' Nene said. "She scored the highest marks in the last biology test.' ‘I know, her aunt said, gloomily, but its "Erdoo this' or ‘Miss Novi that" or women's rights and whatever else from morning till night. I wish she were more like other girls her age. I don't like it." ‘I wouldn't worry, Ma. Efua's different and she's all right the way she is. I think I've offended her; could you please tell her I'm sorry. ‘No problem, dear. I suppose I should be glad she's settled and doing very well. Maybe it's because I no know book. She laughed a little. Back in her room at home, Nene opened her textbook and a small dark booklet dropped out. Curious, she opened it. It was full of Efua's handwriting. On a page there was some poetry: I am a sorry flower A damaged plant I don't know where- It stopped. It didn't make much sense. She turned to the next page. Today I have fallen in love. Diary, can you believe it? I thought I was frozen and love was a silly figment of foolish romance paperbacks. Does it matter who or what you fall in love with? This is something greater than love. It's sublime. It's ecstasy. It was Efua's diary! Nene closed it, thinking she shouldn't be reading it, but something drew her to it. Efua of all people in love! Nene giggled to herself a little. Amazing! A loose page peeked out and Nene pulled it out. It was an attempt at a letter: Darling

Erdoo, when you told me you were leaving, I cannot describe the utter blackness that enveloped me. I will not shy away from it any longer and I don't care what people may say or think. My Erdoo, Miss Novi, mine. Whenever we talk and hug each other I believe I'm in heaven. You are the most fascinating woman in the world- What? Nene was shaking. It must be a mistake of a sort. She had misinterpreted what she had read. It was all very innocent really. Love. We hug. My Erdoo. Efua and Miss Novi? That strange corper with her jeans and short haircut? Could Efua really be a-? No, surely not. She put the booklet back into the book and closed her eyes. *** It was raining so the students couldn't go home straight away. Instead, they hung about talking, mostly about tutorials and the upcoming examinations. Nene was standing in the corridor, staring at the rain, deep in thought. 'Hi, Nens.' It was Jimi. Kobo for your thoughts."

‘Hi,' she said, trying to sound bright. ‘Chin up. Where is your girlfriend, Efua?" ‘I don't know. She's your classmate, not mine. Since discovering the diary, Nene had avoided Efua, trying to think of what to do. ‘She's probably with her other girlfriend, Miss Novi Nene stiffened. Very funny She noticed the rain had stopped Jimi. I think I'll be going now ‘Let's go together. Shall we wait for fua? He always manages to bring everything back to Efua, the thought. Why do you like her so much? What's the matter with you boys? Why? Why? She doesn't even care about you Nene suddenly made up her mind. 'Jimi, Efus is our friend right? And friends always help each other? ‘Yes, you did with me.' ‘Well, I think Efua needs us now and I'm going to show you something You're not to tell anybody. Plcasc, promise ‘1 promise. What is it?' Nene wanted to say 'swear it' but she knew people weren’t supposed to swear. 'Okay, look at this."

She gave Jimi the sheet that contained the letter. He looked at it for such a long time that she said, 'Well? How can we help Her?' ‘Help" he said in a strangled voice. Jimi struggled to say more, then stopped. Without another word, he turned and walked away Nene called out to him, but he didn't wait for her. Suddenly, she felt a little frightened.

CHAPTER 14

It was just before assembly and a crowd had gathered in front of the senior classrooms. Pupils were chattering excitedly, some whispering furiously, some laughing and shaking their heads. Then, Efua walked through the school gates and there was a sudden hush. She stopped, noticing that some students were pointing at her and making furtive gestures. What could be the matter? Joke came running to meet her. 'Efua, don't what's happened?' 'What?' 'Some students are saying some things about...about you and Miss Novi! Some really terrible things about both of you!' Efua went still. Joke continued. 'When I got to school this morning, the boys from arts class were laughing and making rude jokes. Of course, I thought those boys were just fooling around the way they usually do until I heard that there's a letter-supposedly written by you-to that corper.

I think that there's a photocopy or something, because I saw some science students looking over something also. I didn't see it, though!' Joke added hastily. She lowered her voice to a horrified whisper. 'they said you wrote that you were...lovers! That you kiss and hug and-oh I don't know what else to say! Caro today was just laughing and laughing. I don't believe any of it, of course.' There was a roaring sound in Efua's ears. She tried to talk normally but her voice came out in a quavering whisper, 'Did you say...a letter?' She stopped, her heart pounding. Joke stared at her for a moment. I don't believe any of she said again, but this time it sounded as if she was trying to convince herself. Efus, I think you should stay away from classes today.' The news had spread rapidly among the senior students and embellishments had been added along the way, Eiua Coke and Miss Novi. It was the most deliciously horrifying thing to happen to Forcados in a long time. It was there in sow handwriting, 'Can you imagine? You can never trust girls-only sched 'No wonder she never looks at boys... 'I knew there was something wrong with her. Poor Jimi, almost feel sorry for him.' When Nene saw people reading the letter, she almost fainted She immediately went in search of Jimi. "How could you? 'It wasn't... 'Oh don't lie. I showed you something in private and you circulated it to the whole school. I never knew you could be so monstrous!" Then she waved her hands in the air. "God, please forgive me!'

****

There was such an uproar among the senior students that the principal was forced out of his office by the noise. 'What's the matter? Mr. Mallum demanded as he entered the nearest senior class. 'We don't really know, sir, the head girl, Ada, said.

It seems Efua Coker wrote a letter to the corper. I haven't seen it, but some boys in the arts class have it. Let me go and get it from them. When Mr. Mallum saw the letter, which appeared to be the original, he seized it at once and instructed the head boy and head girl to bring any copies they could find to his office immediately. Then, he sent for Efua Coker. Efua was throwing up in the girl's toilet when Ada came looking for her. Calm down, Efua, this isn't the worst thing that has happened Mrs. Tanimoro, the guidance counsellor whose mouth was to you. It isn't. It isn't, she thought as she sat before Mr. Mallum, twisted in self-righteous horror, and the vice principal. Efua imagined what was going through their minds. Oh immorality! Shocking! I always knew she was a bad girl! Bad girl... 'Now, Coker, did you write this letter? the principal asked. Efua bent her head. 'Yes, sir. Mr. Mallum shook his head. 'I should dismiss this, but some of the children are saying some damaging things and it concerns a teacher. There are some things written that are, er, disquieting, you understand?" 'It's not true sir, it's not what it seems. We are very fond of each other of course, but...' ‘Fond of each other?' Mr. Mallum's voice became colder. ‘Please explain yourself. Efua said nothing and the principal sighed. 'I think we need to send for your teacher. You stay here." When Miss Novi came, she hesitated at the doorway. She seemed confused by the trio who sat in stony silence as Efua stood in front of Mr. Mallum's desk. ‘Now Miss Agbenenovi, do you know what is going on?" the principal asked without preamble. 'No, not really, the corper said. ‘It appears you are the object of affection of young Miss Coker here. She also claims you are "very fond of each other". Can you please clarify that?' The corper glanced at Efua before speaking, Efua Coker is interested in some of the extracurricular activities which involve charity work. I introduced her to a few and she has been a very dedicated volunteer. 'I'm sure she is, the principal said dryly. What I mean is, has er...er.... the principal scratched his head, looking for the right words. Efua watched all of them as if in a dream, her head burning. Has there been any improper relationship between the two of you?" The corper whipped her head up. 'Absolutely not, sir!' She was indignant. 'Well, I have a letter here where she writes of you in an... er…,' Indiscreet manner. She writes that you...embrace each other. This is a serious thing, Miss Agbenenovi, I know you will soon be leaving for a new station for the remainder of your service year, but we take a dim view of teachers embracing students Do you do other things? I know young women sometimes er-er wish to experiment...Have you...' Elua gave a strangled shriek. 'Sir, it was nothing like that! They were just-it was just thoughts!' All eyes turned to the distraught girl. Mrs. Tanimoro shook her head disapprovingly. The corper quickly spoke, I'm-I'm embarrassed, sir. I consider Efua Coker as a student, nothing more. She's an enthusiastic volunteer, but clearly confused and disturbed. She's just a young girl. The principal said sternly. In any case, you ought to have known better. You seem to have been more familiar with your students than is to be expected for a teacher, but you'll be excused as you are still very inexperienced.' The principal quickly turned to Efua. ‘You may leave my office. You are excused from school for the rest of today. I would like to see your mother or guardian as soon as possible. Efua came out of the office, weeping. She stopped when she saw Jimi passing by on his way to class. 'Jimi,' she called, relieved. Can you imagine what they're saying about my letter? Why would people think-?' ‘I don't know what to think. You wrote it,' Jimi said, cutting her off. 'Jimi,' she said wearily, 'you don't understand.' 'I read the letter and then someone stole it from me, he said. 'Nene actually saw it first and she didn't know what to think either. The only thing I'm sorry about is that the whole school knows." She went silent. 'You...you hid your true self under a façade,' he said quietly. 'And what if I did? What business is it of yours?" she said, suddenly angry. 'It's none of my business! I hope you two are happy,' he said, just as angrily, and he turned to walk away. It was cruel of him, he knew, but she had made a complete fool of him. I'm proud to have known a person like her!' she called after him. 'You and her, do you know what that means?' He stopped, but did not turn to look at her. 'Yes, and I don't care! She's ten times the person you or anyone else here could ever be. He winced at her words, but by the time he turned to face her, she was gone.

Chapter 15

The next day Mr. Mallum gathered the senior student together. He told them he was shocked by the whole episode- but he was even more shocked by the students' behaviour. He pointed out that Efua Coker was a fellow student who did deserve to be treated like an outcast, and Miss Novi should have been respected as a teacher. ‘Your behaviour has been shameful and disgraceful,' he said. Nobody stirred. They all bent their heads. 'Now, Jolly Stephens, come out!' The matter was explained: Jolly had been rummaging through Jimi's locker, trying to find an assignment he wanted to copy, when he came across Efua's letter. Out of a malicious desire to humiliate Efua, he had made photocopies of the letter and showed them to some other boys. ‘Disgraceful behaviour! How would you like everyone to know your personal thoughts?' said the principal. "This will be the end of the matter.' He proceeded to have Jolly publicly flogged with ten strokes of the cane.

***

Efua's mother arrived at the principal's office with Efua and her aunt. They had met her at the airport and driven straight down. No words had been exchanged. 'Mr.

Mallum, I'm dreadfully sorry about the whole matter,' Mrs. Coker began. It's has been a shock," he said. Such a thing has never been ported in my school before. I'm thankful that nothing-or bast there is no evidence that anything-happened. I care school, and its reputation. '1 do apologise, and I know how stubborn my daughter can be Mrs. Coker gave him a winning smile. Please just let her to the end of term--that dreadful corper must be at fault Thank goodness she's been redeployed somewhere else'. Mr. Mallum took a deep breath. 'Now, madam, the corper has denied anything improper. though she admits they were very friendly. I like to think she simply the object of some misplaced affection. However, have cautioned her severely. I recommend that Efua take a week off classes because a lot of unnecessary unpleasantness has occurred. We will deliberate on the matter and then I'll what I can do." 'Thank you sir, and you know just last week my husband talking about donating new computers, too."

***

Back home her mother raged, "This is the worst thing you have done! You incorrigible...' ‘Funmi, do calm down,' Efua's aunt said nervously. 'It isn't true anyway,' Efua cried. 'At least not the way people think it is! ‘When have you ever told the truth?' her mother said.

Efua's aunt was beginning to think that they were talking about something entirely different. Efua lifted her head defiantly and said, I've always told the truth! Harlot! Sick child! What will you do to me next?" Efua made a swaying motion in the doorway as if she was about to fall down. She clutched the doorknob and then left the room, silently. ‘I have to go back, Efua's mother said to her cousin. Keep the informed of any new developments. Efua stayed in her room for the rest of that day, and the maid said you're not eating anything.' Efua turned over in the bed and said nothing. By the third day Efua's aunt was terrified. Efua, do you want to starve yourself to death?' ‘I don't want to eat anything.' ‘God forbid, you shall eat, even if it's by force. Efua's head and bones ached and she kept drifting off to an uneasy sleep, waking up troubled by nightmares. A hard-faced woman sat on the dressing table beside the mirror wearing expensive jewellery and the latest lace material. Just like her mother. It was her mother. I'm not your mother, the woman said in her cold, hand voice. Nobody can love you. You are nothing.' The sneering, purple lips receded amid the smell of strong, spicy perfume. In its place was a horrifyingly masculine smell mixed with cigar smoke. Then, her stepfather was murmuring through big teeth 'Ahhh, Efua come along. Be a good girl...'

She woke up trembling, feeling as if someone was shouting in her ear. They are coming here and they will do bad things to you. Bad things you deserve. She stood up, wobbling, and went out into the sitting room. It was late evening and nobody was in the house. Her forehead was burning and her throat felt cracked and parched. She didn't know when she left the house, but soon she was crossing the street. A thin scatter-haired girl in a damp t-shirt and jeans weaving through the traffic. She stopped and leaned against a street wall and sank down feeling weak. Scattered tins and pieces of rubbish littered the ground. The air was tainted with the strong smell of urine and waste. A sudden screech startled her. She jumped up. A bedraggled cat crouched in front of her, the fur on its back standing on end. The cat hissed and spat, its eyes glowing. She shrieked and stumbled away, falling among the tins. A voice spoke, ‘Who be dat? Efua looked up; it was a woman. A woman bound up in rags with dirty hair matted together. She was holding a burning tin bmp A mad woman, Efua knew. ‘You, the woman said in a cracked voice. Are you my daughter?’ Efua tried to speak but she wasn't sure. Who am I? Am I her daughter? ‘Sit down, my daughter, sit,’ the woman crooned. ‘Sit down and I will take care of you.’ Efua felt a shudder of revulsion as the woman touched her face; her hand felt scaly, like a lizard. The woman began to chant and mutter meaningless words and Efua slowly drifted asleep. When she woke up she found herself in a room surrounded by people in white and she gasped. ‘She's awake.’ It was her aunt's voice. ‘Thank God! Efua you are in hospital. ‘Thank God, another voice said. "Ah Efua,' her aunt said, stroking her head. "Don't do this to me again. Thank God you didn't wander too far off. We found you unconscious on the streets of Lagos! A young girl! You are safe now. Rest.' She understood that, but where was the old witch, the one who said she was her mother? She could hear the doctor saying severe malaria' and she leaned back against the pillows. It was good to be here, away from everybody. She wanted to be somewhere safe.

Chapter 16

Nene felt thoroughly empty and guilty. She couldn't do anything, not even pray. She was silent while helping her mother prepare dinner. 'Nene, what is the matter?' ‘It's Efua. She's ill and unhappy and it's all my fault.' ‘Your fault? ‘Yes, I was trying to help her, at least I said I was, but mother...I don't know.' Her mother dried her hands. 'Nene, talk to me." Nene's voice went flat. 'I was jealous of her. She's so attractive and boys always become silly over her. Jimi, Ansa...and she had helped Jimi so much. They seemed to talk of nothing but Efua, Efua...I just thought "What's so special about her?" You know, I think that because I was jealous, I showed Jimi the letter. Because I... I think I wanted him to see her for what she was and like her much less. Maybe because I... I wanted him just to look at me too. Can you imagine?' Her mother was silent. ‘I'm a monster,' Nene sobbed. 'Can't you say anything?' Her mother sighed. What do you want me to say? How do you feel now?'

‘Terrible. I didn't know everybody would see it. I miss her. ‘I'm so confused.' ‘You have to go and see her and explain everything. Including your part.' ‘I can't go and see her,' Nene wailed. 'If you are truly her friend you will go and see her. I'll buy some things for you to take along. Come on.

***

Efua sat up in the hospital bed; she was feeling much better. Some people had sent gifts and cards. Ansa had designed a special one shaped like a large bouquet of flowers. Her school friends from St Catherine's had also sent a card, collectively signed with hearts and kisses. How did they know she was here? There was also a letter from her former principal sending warm thoughts and wishing her the best in life. She smiled sadly. What a mess she had made of her life. ‘Hello Efua,' a voice spoke. She looked up, it was Nene. ‘How are you?' Nene came forward smiling nervously. I’ve missed you. Everybody has. I've baked you a cake. Did you ger-‘ ‘What do you want? Doesn't it offend your pure and gentle soul to be sitting beside me?" ‘Efua, I'm really sorry.' She sat on the bed. 'I-I saw the letter by accident and showed Jimi. I didn't know anybody else would find out... I don't think Jimi did either.'

‘Yes I know, you wanted to help me.' Efua looked away. I'm a dreadful person. I'm not fit to be beside someone like you, so just go and leave me alone.' Nene took a deep breath. I have a confession to make. 1-I did it on purpose. I showed Jimi the letter because I was jealous of you’. Efua raised her head, astonished. Jealous? Of what?" ‘Of you, everything you are. You can see what sort of person I am; not half as good as you because I pretended to myself,

I was trying to help you. Efua, I don't care what people think you are. I love you as a sister and I still want to be your friend, if you'll let the. Can you ever find it in your heart to forgive me?' Edua said nothing and Nene continued, feeling desolate I'm very, very, sorry and I understand if you hate me now, but I'll never give up on our friendship' She stood up and twisted her hands. I'm sorry, Nene repeated. I'll come over to see you tomorrow.' She turned to go. 'Nene, wait,' Efua said. married my stepfather when I was twelve. She said it would Efua started talking in an expressionless voice. 'My mother give us a better life after my father died. It wasn't so bad at first bully. Luckily except for his- his son. He was a nasty, mean he was away most of the time. Efua made a gulping sound, shuddering. "Then when I was thirteen, he-my stepfather- became worse.

He started making immoral suggestions, but I pretended as if I didn't understand what he was saying. Sometimes, he'd grab me... touching me...it was so sickening. Then he came to my room one night and-and he made me do things to him. He'd put his...' She stopped. Nene was wide-eyed with shock. Efua continued. 'He threatened to kill me if I told anyone. He did it several times. Last year, he came to my room again and then I knew I couldn't take it anymore. I fought back with a knife. He was badly hurt. Nene was shaking her head with horror. Efua was crying now. "Nobody believed me and my mother called me a demon- possessed liar! She said I was trying to ruin her marriage. I don't blame her. I can't forget. I get nightmares and I see him there. I keep wishing it all never happened. I was so scarcd that's why I... I stabbcd him,' shc sobbcd. 'About Miss Novi, she was just a nice, lovely friend. Nothing went on and now she thinks I'm a bad person. I always destroy people's lives! 'Don't you see, it's me...I'm filthy. There must be something about me that makes men and boys want to do those things to me. It's me!' 'It wasn't your fault!' Nene cried. She held Efua and cried a little, too. 'Do you know what, Efua? People may fail you-I did-but God loves you, honestly he does. It may not be much, but I love you too. And you know, you're going to be a great person inspite of all you've been through and once you've recovered…' Efua shuddered. 'I really can't go back to that school." 'You can. I'll help you. I'll be right there beside you.' She smiled and squeezed her hand. Efua sniffed and tried to smile swell. Nene hugged her tightly. 'So let's go and show them.'

Chapter 17

Back in his home, Jimi lay on his bed staring at the ceiling. The house was empty for once. It had become a little difficult staying with Ansa who was now finding fault with him out how had treated Efua. 'Ansa, I'm sorry I said those things to her, but I thought she liked me-until I saw that letter,' Jimi had said earlier. ‘Well, I'm her friend, if you can understand that, and I don't like the way you behaved,' said Ansa. ‘Look at her and how she used to treat me, she deceived us. ‘Jimi, think about how she acted when you had trouble with your brother, Ansa said, risking a punch. 'She was your friend, but were you ever her friend?" Jimi was stricken at Ansa's words. Nene was no longer talking to him and, for the first time he could remember, Ansa was not taking his side. He stared at the ceiling trying not to think about her. What was she doing? How was she feeling? He kept trying to push her out of his mind, but her face kept appearing. If he went to see her what would she say? 'Down with love,' he muttered.

‘Then Wole came in. "Hey Jims-what are you doing here? ‘What do you mean? It's my house as much as yours. ‘Oh well, great of you to finally remember you have a brother.' Wole sat on the bed and Jimi studied him. For once his brother was not smiling and he looked nervous and jerky. 'Wole, what's wrong?" No answer. Jimi sat up. "Wole, is it the bad stuff? I told you... ‘No, not that. Jimi, I'm in trouble. Deep trouble. ‘Wh-what is it?’ Wole's eyes were haunted. I need money, lots of it. ‘What have you done this time? ‘I needed some cash so I helped some guys to sell some things. I just didn't sell enough. ‘What did you sell? ‘You know...’ ‘You sold drugs? Did you run away with their money? ‘You can't judge me. Wole turned his face and Jimi saw that was bruised and swollen. ‘Your face. What happened?' ‘I came across some of the guys today, said Wole. "They aren't joking. Look Jims, my life could be in danger.’ Jimi's blood ran cold and he felt sick. ‘I'll give you all the money I have. Maybe we could go and see Uncle K?' ‘No, Wole said. "Thing is, I might not even be safe here tonight."

‘What about your friends? Can't they help?' ‘Friends?' His brother laughed grimly and then yelped in pain. ‘Wole, what are you going to do?' Jimi said. ‘I have to get away tonight, that's how bad things are." ‘Wole, you know I'd do anything for you, but will things be okay?' stop there? Will you ‘Fine, I'll be fine.' He gave Jimi a hug. 'Get some money for me and pack some of your shirts for me. And your watch. ‘My watch?' ‘Bro, I'll make it up to you. I swear it.' *** Later when they were at the bus stop, Jimi asked, "When will you be back?' ‘As soon as I'm somewhere safe I'll call you so you can help me get the rest of the money. Dad or Uncle K will give it to you if you can tell a good lie. Okay?' Wole said. 'I know I've been a total creep and I don't deserve you, but whatever is going to happen, just know I never meant anything. I swear it. You'll always be my little brother.' He hesitated. Bye, he added quickly before walking into the darkness. As he watched Wole go, Jimi had a sudden memory of when the two of them were small and Wole was teaching him how to ride a bicycle for the first time. 'I can't,' Jimi had sobbed after falling off the bicycle for the fifth time. 'Yes you can,' Wole had said. "See, I can stand and cycle and you can too. I promise.' Jimi had. That was his Wole. Whatever anyone said, it had always been both of them against the world. That night, Jimi could not sleep. He thought of his mother and badly wished she were here. 'Look after your brother, she had said. But Jimi was the younger one and now he needed looking after himself.

Chapter 18

Jimi heard the news when he got back to school on Monday Morning. ‘Jimi, did you hear? Seyi, the head boy said. "The lab has been broken into! The new microscope and other stuff have been stolen! Jimi ran to the laboratory. Mr. Edet was there and so were the two lab technicians. The chemistry teacher wrung has hands. Jimi felt sorry for him and angry as well was a clean job, done by someone who had access to the key, one of the technicians was saying Mr. Edet looked beaten. In spite of all we've done! We lobbied so hard before we were able to raise funds for the equipment. You were part of it, Jimi, remember? Running up and down from one office to the other. I gave you the other key on Friday-when you science students had the after-class tutorial, didn't I? Where is it?" ‘In my bag, Jimi opened his bag. He couldn't find it He rummaged frantically. He had put it there on

Friday. He searched but an ugly, cold feeling was rising inside him 'I can't...maybe it's at home or something'

The teacher observed him strangely. You'll have to get it as soon as possible today. 'Yes sir.'

***

That morning, Efua returned to school, with Nene walking dose beside her. They ignored the buzz of gossip and it was only Jolly who bent his head and stumbled a little when he saw her Nene was fiercely protective all day.' 'Just keep ignoring anybody who tries to say anything nasty I'll report anyone who harasses you to the principal, she said. Ansa came to meet them. Welcome Efua, we all missed you!' 'Thanks,' she said and her eyes moistened a little. During break Jimi went over to her. Hello Efua.' She raised her face to him and then turned back to her book. I'm, I'm -gosh, Efua-

I'm sorry.' She raised her face to him again and said "There's nothing to be sorry about. I'd like you to go away, please." His ears burned as he walked away. Passing a table, he heard a malicious titter. It was Caro sitting with her group. He had completely forgotten there were mean people like Caro around.

***

Later, lost in his worries about the missing key, Jimi bumped into Nene. 'Nene, I'm sorry about everything, Please listen, I'm sorry! She sighed, 'Let's forget it. It wasn't your fault. It was mine." 'How is she? 'She's okay. 'I said terrible things to her. I'm trying to apologise but she won't...?' 'Jimi, I think the best thing is if you stay away from her for now. Best not to upset her. 'I know I'm not her favourite person, but if you could talk to her..." 'I'll say something, but Jimi, if you upset her, I'll be very angry. I'm not joking' She walked away with a throwaway. 'Hope things are going okay for you.' But things weren't. A sick gnawing feeling kept biting the pit of his stomach. He skipped the rest of the day's classes and went home to search for the key. He couldn't find it. even though he almost tore the whole place down. Suddenly a strange thought floated into his mind. Wole. He killed the shameful thought at once. Wole didn't know anything about the laboratory, or Forcados for that matter. He sat down in the of his room and buried his face in his hands, trying to think of what to do.

***

The next day as Jimi arrived at school, the principal sent for him. Mr. Mallum was standing with Mr. Edet. They were not smiling. 'The key, Solade. You were the last person to have it, weren't you?' said Mr. Mallum. 'Yes sir, but I can't find it. I must have misplaced it and I take the blame... The principal interrupted him. 'Do you know who could have taken it?'

'N-no.' 'The principal looked at him for a moment before he said, 'We've caught the thieves.' Jimi felt relieved. Thieves. "Who? Petty burglars?" I'm afraid not. A certain Wole Solade and some other boys were trying to sell the equipment when the police caught them. He says he's your brother. Jimi's heart sank to the bottom of his shoes. "That's not all. He claims you let him in, showed him the equipment and masterminded the whole thing. We are going to the police station."

***

It didn't take long for the news to spread around the school: Jimi Solade, health prefect and school hero was being questioned in the police station over missing laboratory equipment. The school was struck dumb.

Chapter 19

Jimi lay slumped on his bed, but he couldn't sleep. His brain was filled with voices saying this and that. He had gone to the police station. It was a filthy, rundown place with broken benches, stinking of unwashed bodies and human waste; the kind of place that was used to house seedy criminals. He saw Wole in a cell behind the counter staring back at him with a sick expression on his face. He tried to ignore the scruffy policemen saying things like: ‘Hey, boy, is it true you and your brother take gbana?' ‘You did all that at your age." ‘Young boys of nowadays.' He had stayed there, on a bench by the door, until the principal contacted their uncle and Wole was granted bail. When they had a private moment together, just before Jimi left with Uncle Kazeem, Wole had whispered, Jimi, just do this for me. I didn't mean it. I didn't know they were from your school. With your clean record your principal would pardon you, while they'll lock me up for years. Just say you did it and gave me the items. The lawyer can think up something. Please Jimi, my brother, beg your principal. Do you want me locked up for years?" He knew what had happened. His brother must have known it was Jimi's school. He had masterminded the whole thing and stolen the key to get access to the lab. But had it been Wole's fault? Surely not. It was the fault of the drugs and the fact that their dad didn't care, wasn't it? And so, he had said yes to the police. It was true. He, Jimi, had broken into the lads. The teachers were shocked. Even the principal had believed him. Somehow it made things seem much less terrible - or more. 'Jimi Solade, I'm expressing my profound disappointment. I'm appalled,' Mr. Malbum said. 'You were one of my golden students. You were a role model.' They decided not to press charges against him and, after much deliberation, allowed him to take his end-of-term exams, but as a separate student, away from everyone else. Everyone whispered about him as he walked around like a pariah, carrying out the punishment of cutting grass. He tried ore them and concentrate on his studies instead Most of his friends avoided him, except Ansa who came to him at once. Jimi, what happened? ‘You know what happened.

‘I've heard what they're saying but what really happened? ‘You heard what happened," he said again. Ansa gulped. Nene also came. I don't want to believe it. I'll be praying for you she said sincerely He thought of Efua and how she must have felt when everyone was gossiping about her. Now, here he was with his mother gone, his father not around and everybody hating him. At least his brother would be all right, so it was all worth it-wasn't it?

***

After the long-awaited WAEC exams, the senior students of Forcados were free to do what they wanted-all except Jimi Solade. He was banned from all social activities and he was going to have to publicly apologise to the whole school. ‘That is the least you can do, Mr. Mallum had said. ‘I'm really sorry, sir, Jimi had said. ‘Not as sorry as I am, the principal had said sadly. On that day, he made sure his school uniform was very neat. He had already handed over his prefect's badge. It was not a cold morning, but he felt chilly. All the students were walking towards the hall, he saw Efua and Nene walking together. He hesitated and then went over to them. 'Efua, Nene! ‘Hello Nene was about to say more, then she stopped and quietly excused herself, leaving him alone with Efua. ‘Hello, Efna, he said.

'Hello, Jimi He had forgotten about the butterflies in his stomach. 'Elua, I know you think I'm getting what I deserve now, but I'm just asking you not to have a bad impression of me. I'm not the same person I was.' He wished he could express himself better and that she would say something instead of staring at him as if he were an alien. I'm really sorry and, whatever it means to you, I did like you, I really did.' She opened her mouth as if she wanted to say something. but then the teachers were calling and everyone was hurrying into the hall, so he turned and walked away. Efua joined Nene. 'What did he say?" Efua looked straight ahead. 'He said he was sorry about everything.' 'Poor Jimi. 'I didn't know what to say. "You deserve it?" 'Efua, Nene sighed and patted her hand. 'Sorry, but I'm not a nice person.' The teachers were seated on chairs on stage. When the principal lifted his microphone, the hum and chatter gradually died down. 'We are here to listen to one of us speak. Solade, come up." Jimi gripped the microphone. Five hundred bright-eyed students stared back at him. His hands were sweating, but his voice was clear. 'Dear fellow students, you all know why I'm here; I've come to apologies. I have no excuses; I was wrong and I'm pleading...'

When he'd finished, he was surprised at how calm he felt. 'Very good,' the principal said. "Now I would plead with all of you to accept his apology. He has served and is serving his punishment. And it nothing else, it shows courage. Suddenly a voice spoke up. Excuse me sir, can I say something! was Efua. The principal looked at her nonplussed and then he nodded. There was already a hum rising, but she walked up to the stage anyway What did she want to say? Jimi wondered. Surcly, she didn't want to add more salt to his wounds? She glanced at him and then said in her cool, deep voice. a good thing that the equipment was recovered and then culprit or culprits were found. But sir, do you think this is right. 'What do you mean?" the principal asked, frowning a little. 'Well sir, here is your student, a student whom you known since he started junior secondary school. Who you and the other teachers judged was worthy to be made a prefect in his final year. Yet, when something like this happened, you didn't wonder how it was possible. You didn't think that maybe there was a big mistake made somewhere? Or even if he did do this terrible thing; did you even try to find out why?" ‘Miss Coker,' the principal said coldly, 'can you please get to the point?

There was a rising hum among the students in the hall. This was sounding interesting. My question to you sir, is how well do you know your students and how much do you really care about them? What is more important to you: the lost equipment, the fine standards of your school, or the students in your care? Your star student supposedly admitted to stealing laboratory equipment, but why? What would make him do such a thing! Has he ever done something like that before! Efua's voicc rose. Why do you always want to believe the worst about people? She stopped and panted a little. Then she went on softly. 'I'm sorry sit, but you don't care enough. It is easy to judge others and to cast stones. You arc the teacher, sir-someone examine yourself, what is the right thing in this case? Have you really acted out of love for this boy? I challengc you to investigate the matter again. I think you will then be able to see a victim. The principal was stunned.

'Coker, I don't know what you hope to achieve. He may be your friend-' Then Ansa stood up. Quiet, shy Ansa, who had never spoken in public before. He shouted for the whole hall to hear, 'It can't be Jimi. It was his brother; he's only taking the blame for him!' There was dead silence and then one person started clapping and then another and another. Soon the whole school was applauding. Jimi stood with his mouth open, staring at Efua. He couldn't believe it. She looked at him for a moment full in the face. He suddenly thought: You stood up for me and I didn't do that for

You, and his eyes up filled And then all the pent-up emotion up poured out and he was crying unashamedly. He forgot to be collected and cool. He forgot he was in front of the whole school. 'Solade. To my office,' the principal said. 'I'll see all of you in exactly an hour.' Jimi told him everything. 'It was a foolhardy thing to do,' the principal said. 'Why didn't you just tell me everything? I would have helped you.' Jimi swallowed. They went to the police station. There the thieves confessed everything. Wole sat in silence. He gazed at something unseen on the ground and did not speak, even when Mr. Mallum said, 'You should be ashamed of yourself doing that to your own brother!' ‘Please sir, you don't understand,' Jimi said. I know what you're thinking, but he's my brother. I'm all he's got and he's all that I've got!' There was a long silence. ‘Jimi?' Mr. Mallum finally said. It was the first time he had addressed a student by his first name. 'Yes?' ‘I'm sorry. I was not perceptive enough to see the truth.' He turned to Wole. I'm going to drop all of the charges against you. Not because you deserve it, but because I'm sorry for you.'

***

When Jimi got back to school his mind was strangely empty. He met Nene and Ansa privately while Mr. Mallum addressed the whole school again. 'I didn't deserve this from you,' said Jimi to his friends. ‘Who deserves anything?' Nene said, murmuring to herself. ‘It's like grace. God's grace. After they hugged each other, he said, with attempted nonchalance, 'Where's Efua?' 'Er... Nene said, 'She's gone. She told me that after that issue with Miss Novi, her mother made arrangements for her to leave the country after she finished her exams. She must have come to school specially for this.' 'She's gone?' He stood still, shocked. ‘I’m sorry Jimi, but at least you'll always remember what she did.' 'She was magnificent!' Ansa said dreamily. 'Jims, aren't you the lucky one!' ‘She didn't change till the end, he wanted to shout, but he kept quiet and they walked inside the hall.

Chapter 20

It was October and the results were out. The graduated students milled about the school grounds, dressed in mufti. Some had come with their parents. Most people in the year had performed brilliantly, particularly Jimi Solade. He had won a scholarship to study electrical engineering. During the valedictory service that had been held in July he had collected prizes in chemistry, physics and technical drawing. Nene had done well also; she was hoping to study accountancy. Ansa too, had made his papers. 'I'll study architecture," he had announced happily when he got his results. I'll always be an artist.' The principal had beamed at all of them saying, I'm very proud of you all.' Jimi was thinking about other matters. He thought of the past year in which so much had happened. What were the things that really mattered? he wondered. Jimi, I'm proud of you, Mr. Mallum had said. It was the same thing the principal always said. Same thing, but a different Jimi now. Shortly after she left, Efua had sent him a letter. Dear Jimi, Funny how I can be writing to you, but I hope everything turned out right. It may not have been my business, but I couldn't just sit there and let someone who was innocent take the blame. I always believed you were innocent. I'm doing okay here and I'm looking forward to getting into university to study medicine. could things have been different I don't know. You remember what you said to me last that day? Well. I'm telling you feel just the same. But I believe people need to sort out things inside themselves first, and I'm trying. All the same, I want you to know that what you tried to do for your brother was wonderful. Brave! It was the sweetest thing. You're going to be someone special someday. Efua The sweetest thing! That was the kind of thing a girl would write. Would he ever understand girls? He knew he'd probably never see her again, but he would never stop thinking about her, especially that image of her angelic face with her long hair flowing out beneath her school cap that night when they walked home together, or that day when she sat with him at his mother's funeral. Yet, it hurts to say her name, to even think about her Funny how someone can make you feel both happy and sad at the same time, he thought. Ansa came over. What a year!' 'Yes'. And for no reason at all, they burst out laughing. 'Why are you laughing? Ansa said between gulps. 'Why are you laughing?" said Jimi. They laughed so hard that tears started to fall. People started. wondered, and then smiled at the two boys.

THE END

THE AUTHOR

O.B Adewale is a Lagosian and this book is his first book.